Here's What People Are Saying About
"FIGHTING BACK"
and Keith Deltano

Keith has a straightforward approach for parents. He doesn't sugar coat anything. The reproducible section is a great idea and I'm sure parents will find it useful.

Tammy Beardsley
South Valley Pregnancy Care Center
A CareNet Affiliate
Morgan Hill, CA

Remarkable! Mr. Deltano has created a guide that allows the average parent to cut through the confusion and take action!

Dr. Johnnie Gordon
Public School Principal
Charlotte, NC

As a Family Connection director and as a parent, I loved the book!!! The book is parent friendly. Keith does much more than present the problem, he gives parents the information and tools they need to fight back.

Donna B. Barrett
Habersham County Connection
Clarksville, GA

I consider Mr. Deltano to be one of the most innovative and effective teachers I have known in the twenty years I have spent in Teacher Education.

David Strahan, Ed.D.
Associate Professor
University of North Carolina

"FIGHTING BACK" educates and empowers parents to connect with their teens to reinforce the positive message of abstinence.

Julie Schrieber
Director, Care Net Pregnancy Center
Ladysmith, WI

"FIGHTING BACK" ... I couldn't put it down once I started reading it. It is so effective because Keith writes in an easy to understand style and guides the reader through a step-by-step approach that can immediately be put into practice.

Dawn Porter
Parent of teens
Hillsdale, PA

continued to next page . . .

I'm not a "reader." But after taking a quick look (at my wife's request) I felt compelled to read and implement the chapters that spoke directly to my responsibilities as a father and "Dad."

Frank Starr
NASCAR team coordinator
and Parent of four girls
Greensboro, NC

Your message, "Abstinence is Cool," was energetic, hard-hitting, easy to understand and captivating. We are thankful for the many commitments to virginity we had that day.

Suncoast Association
Largo, FL

I highly recommend Mr. Keith Deltano to any school or civic group. I have been in education over 30 years, and few assemblies have moved the students as well as your presentation on abstinence.

Jerry Srur, Principal
North Central Of Barnes
Rogers, ND

The leaders in attendance were thrilled with the response of their youth and we extend their overwhelming positive feedback.

Doug Petty, Director
Cove Camp
Asheville, NC

"FIGHTING BACK" educates and empowers parents to connect with their teens to reinforce the positive message of abstinence. Thanks for caring about kid's, Keith.

Leslee J. Unruth, Founder and President
Abstinence Clearinghouse
Sioux Falls, SD

Keith's book is a testament to the years he has spent working with teens and families. I hope that many parents will be inspired to enact his suggestions.

Pamela J. Roebuck
Assistant State Attorney
Stuart, Florida

FIGHTING BACK

How to Promote Abstinence in a Sex-saturated World

Keith Deltano
Author, Teacher and Educational Comedian

About the Author

Keith Deltano has served and worked with young people as a military police officer, public school teacher, youth leader, private counselor, and educational comedian and storyteller. Keith draws on this varied background and first hand experience to reach out and share with youth and educate parents.

After three years in the military police, Keith attended the University of North Carolina at Greensboro and graduated with a Bachelor of Science degree in Elementary Education. Keith taught sixth grade from 1990 until 1996. He is a winner of the Teacher Excellence Award and listed in Outstanding Young Men of America and Who's Who of American Teachers. In 1996 he went into full time family coaching and youth speaking. He currently runs Freedom Entertainment with his wife Julia, and also maintains a small caseload of families with children that are struggling academically or behaviorally. Julia and Keith have two young children.

This book will help you create an environment, within this sex-saturated world, where virginity *is* possible.

The focus of this book is simple. *FIGHTING BACK* gives parents strategies and insight on how to insure their child's virginity (or reclaim that virginity) throughout the teen years. *FIGHTING BACK* promotes abstinence until marriage and monogamy afterward. This book assumes that the reader believes that sex should be a fulfilling experience that takes place between a married man and woman and that teenage experimentation, whether "protected" or "unprotected," can only leave physical, emotional or spiritual scars. This book does not defend the abstinence movement. The writer assumes that you prefer abstinence education to safe sex (unsafe sex) education for your children. However, if you believe that promoting "safe sex" is the answer, please refer to chapter twelve.

Keith can't and won't give a guarantee that the strategies outlined within this book will work for every child and every family. However, when addressing teen sexual behavior, doing something is always better than doing nothing.

FIGHTING BACK

How to Promote Abstinence in a Sex-saturated World

Keith Deltano

Author, Teacher and Educational Comedian

FREEDOM

ENTERTAINMENT
PUBLISHING CO.

Julian, North Carolina 27283

FIGHTING BACK
How to Promote Abstinence in a Sex-saturated World

Published by Freedom Entertainment Publishing Co.
6043 Smithwood Road • Julian, NC 27283
e-mail: delta@vnet.net • www.keithdeltano.com

Printed in the United States of America
First printing 2004

Cover Design by Progressive Media, 2116 Southview Avenue, Tampa, FL 33606
Edited by Keith Deltano

ISBN 0-9718881-2-4

Special Thanks

To all who have supported Julia and me and our dreams with encouragement and enthusiasm.

To Rich Dymmel for hitting the road with me and for helping with research, and to Jerome Renn and Lonnie Baxley for keeping me straight.

To Jeff Triplett for giving me a laptop computer. What was old to him was new to me. Thanks to him I was able to work while, "On the Road." Much of this book has been written (typed) in Waffle Houses and airports around the country.

To Granny Franny and Grampy Grumpy for helping out with the children whenever Julia and I had to focus on "work."

To Larry and Dottie Nylin of Dove Publications and Software for coming forward after a "Keeping Your Kid A Virgin" workshop and offering to donate their publishing, editing and set up skills. Their help and encouragement were pivotal in the production of this book.

To all who have supported and believed in Freedom Entertainment and the idea that comedy can be used to address serious issues.

To Mike Williams, for saying the right things at the right times and for showing that, "it's possible."

To all the families that opened up their homes to me on my travels performing, "Abstinence Is Cool."

To all the schools that let a "comedian" in to teach about abstinence.

To Tim Grable, Ron Miller and the Nashville Speakers Bureau for signing me "on faith" and for taking away much of the office workload so I could focus on the book and have more time for my growing family.

To my Mother for teaching me how to read when the public school system couldn't and to my Dad for teaching me that, "Deltanos never quit."

To Alex and Angie McFarland and Barrett Riddleburger for being able to dream big and see the vision when everyone else thought I was crazy. And for being inspirations by following their own dreams.

To my enduring wife who has stuck with me through countless dreams and misadventures until I found "The Thing" I wanted to do with my life. Thank you for believing in educational comedy and in the book even when times were tight. For being happy with things that really *matter* rather than *things*. For fixing the computer every time I mess it up. Thank You Julia.

What the Meaning of Abstinence Is

It seems that there would be no misunderstanding about this word. But we do live in a time when people ask what the meaning of "is" is. Many groups now promote "abstinence." Some of those same groups condone and encourage condom and pill distribution. Their definition of abstinence is murky at best. Following is the author's understanding and approach to abstinence education:

☆ Abstinence from sex before marriage is not a spur of the moment temporary contraceptive. It is a lifestyle choice that develops strong personality traits that will help an individual throughout life.

☆ Abstinence in this book refers to avoiding sexual intercourse as well as any activity involving genital contact or genital stimulation. *(Yes, oral sex is sex.)*

☆ Being sexually abstinent before marriage increases the probability of pleasurable, fulfilling, and healthy sexual intimacy after marriage.

☆ Individuals who have been sexually active in the past may still chose abstinence and remain abstinent until marriage.

Contents

Introduction

The first three chapters will challenge you to examine what you are thinking and where you stand when dealing with your teenager about sexual issues. The following chapters outline prevention strategies that can be implemented immediately. Keith will start with the easiest intervention strategies and move to the most difficult.

Keith will first ask you, the parent, to examine and perhaps change the way you think. If you want a quick and easy formula for ensuring your child's sexual purity then put this book back. If you are not willing to make changes in your *own* behavior, this book is not for you. The battle for your child's sexual purity starts in *your* head. We will begin by examining how you think, or if you are thinking at all, about your child's sexual worldview.

You cannot afford not to read this book. The strategies outlined within are just too simple to ignore. If you're reading this now, you are probably a woman between the ages of thirty and fifty. Get your husband to read it. Better yet get your husband to read it at the same time and discuss it with him. If you can't do either, then highlight the important part and get him to read that. If all else fails hide the remote until partial compliance occurs and have him sign the Acknowledge of Impact Contract (R.12 in Appendix B).

PART ONE

What Are You Thinking?

The way to be safe is never to be secure.
– Benjamin Franklin

Most of our platitudes notwithstanding,
self-deception remains the most difficult deception.
– Joan Didion

CHAPTER 1

Your Kids Are Safe . . . Aren't They?

The following is a survey you can take to determine if your children are at risk for premarital sexual activity. Please check the appropriate box:

1. Does your child live in America? ❏ Yes ❏ No

2. Is your child between the ages of ten and nineteen? ❏ Yes ❏ No

If you answered "Yes" to both the above questions, then your children are at risk. **That's it, period.** It doesn't matter if you live in a nice neighborhood. It doesn't matter if your children go to church. It doesn't matter if you're a college educated, white, BMW driving country couple. It doesn't matter if you're the Mayor or PTA president. If you answered "Yes" to the above questions, then **your** children are at risk.

The First Thing You Must Do
Is Leave The Comfort Of Denial

Why must a book that has a goal of controlling **your teen's sexual behavior** examine the way **you think?** Because it must. You simply cannot fight against what you do not feel is a threat. You must think about how you think concerning these issues. Why are so many parents in denial about their teen's risk of sexual activity? Why may you be in denial about this topic, reluctant to think about it and even more reluctant to act on it?

- **DENIAL IS COMFORTABLE.** You're pulling in the driveway and you notice your daughter playing in the sprinkler with her friends from down the street. You notice how she has changed in the past few months. She's just started having her period and you're proud of how you handled that. It was a warm mother-daughter moment. It occurs to you that perhaps now is the time to talk to her about other sexual issues. Your stomach churns at the idea. Besides she's only thirteen. That's too young to worry about such things. You pull into the garage thinking about supper and who is running the soccer carpool tonight. Much more comfortable thoughts.

- **DENIAL IS PRIDEFUL.** You're pulling into the driveway and you notice your daughter and her friends toweling off on the front steps. Your son is awkwardly standing on the sidewalk kicking a rock and trying to talk to one of the girls. You feel a twinge of pride as you glance at your daughter. She's become so pretty. Your wife told you that she's started her period. Perhaps you should talk to her about boys and all that. No, you don't have to worry about your daughter becoming sexually active. After all, you've worked hard to live in a good neighborhood and send her to a good school. You've taught right from wrong and set a good example, and with you as her father, well, how could she go wrong? And your son, well you haven't really talked with him. But you know that he knows that you will kill him if he ever gets sexually involved with a girl. That should be enough. You've got everything else so well handled; the issue of teen sexual activity isn't going to enter your home. You swing into the garage rather pleased with yourself and the job you're doing.

- **DENIAL IS OUR FIRST RESPONSE.** Man is a creature of comfort. We crave the easy path. It is more comfortable to deny a problem than to acknowledge it. Why? Because if you admit to the presence of a problem you must choose to respond or not to respond. If you choose to respond then you may have to do something that takes effort or makes you uncomfortable. If you choose not to respond then you are saddled with the guilt of your inaction. Guilt and effort are not comfortable nor pleasant. It is much easier to take the approach that, "It's someone else's kids" or "Not in my house." Denial saves you from effort or guilt but denial cannot save you from the possible and very real consequences of inaction.

Denial is Dangerous

What exactly might you be in denial about? Am I insisting that your children are sexually active and you don't want to admit it? No, of course not. You may be denying even the **possibility** that your children could become sexually active. To be in denial is to ignore or fail to address a problem. Today, promiscuous teen sexual behavior **is** a problem. Your teens may not be sexually active, but they are at risk and you still must face the problem.

Well, what is happening out there? What is happening in your neighborhood, town and state? What is happening to the youth of our country? What is the scope of the problem I'm asking you to face? Let's look at some facts.

In 2002 experts stated that the increasingly early initiation of sexual behavior is taking its toll on teen mental health.[1]

10% of teenage girls have chlamydia. Half of new chlamydia cases occur in girls 15 to 19 years old.[2]

Now, are you ready for a shocker? These next stats should wake you up.

18 percent of 15 year-olds will become mothers before they are out of their teens.[3]

In 2000 10% of sexually active girls will become pregnant[4]

What does this mean for you? Are there ten girls in your neighborhood, extended family or other group? One of them will become pregnant this year. It's that simple. Is this getting any more real for you? It doesn't seem like that many girls are getting pregnant in your area does it? Let's look at a darker side of the statistical equation. Just because 1 out of 10 girls in America are conceiving, does not mean that 1 out of 10 girls are actually giving birth. The 10% conception statistic measures just that: conception. And if you think that these particular researchers are off, they're not. Study after study puts the pregnancy rate for American girls between the ages of 14 and 19 at 10% to 15%.

Now, where are all these pregnant girls and babies in your neighborhood? Where are all these pregnancies?

14 percent of teen pregnancies ended in a miscarriage and 35 percent were terminated by abortion.[5]

That's right, abortion. Many teenaged pregnancies are terminated before parents and community are aware of the conception. What does it tell us about ourselves as a society when roughly 35 percent of teen pregnancies end in abortion? Sadly, unwanted pregnancy and abortion are only part of the price the nation's youth are paying for sex.

One in five children over age 12 tests positive for herpes type 2.[6]

American children are suffering a silent epidemic. Sexually transmitted diseases are affecting children within every demographic group. The above statistics do not come exclusively from at risk populations. The researchers were careful to examine the behavior of teens throughout the socioeconomic spectrum. These are your children. What do we learn about ourselves as a nation when 20% of our young people have a virus that they will have to contend with for the rest of their life? They were told to practice "protected sex." Did we protect them?

The whole intent of this chapter is to get you out of a state of denial, if you're in one. That's it. You can't begin to solve a problem if you refuse to admit there is one. The most dangerous thing you can do is ... NOTHING. Where are you on the following graph?

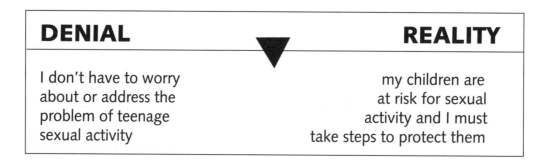

DENIAL		REALITY
I don't have to worry about or address the problem of teenage sexual activity		my children are at risk for sexual activity and I must take steps to protect them

Think about the crew of the Titanic. They were warned about icebergs. Icebergs were known to be in the area of the Atlantic they were steaming. True, the odds of actually hitting one at that time of year were low.

They were comfortable. Never had anyone traveled on the sea in such comfort. They had a gym, a ballroom, fine china, the company of one another. Why should they consider what lay outside the hull of the ship? You too, are comfortable. Never has the American family lived in such splendor and material well being. Why should you consider what lies outside the comfort of your home?

They were proud. They had built the finest ship in the entire world, had they not? She was unsinkable. She had five watertight compartments. She was the largest ship afloat with the finest technology available in her day. Why should they even think about the possibility of hitting an iceberg, much less sinking? You have achieved so much with your home, career, car and family. Why should you waste time taking steps to prevent something that can't happen in your house anyway? You needn't worry about your children becoming sexually active.

They were in denial about the danger that lies ahead. Are You?

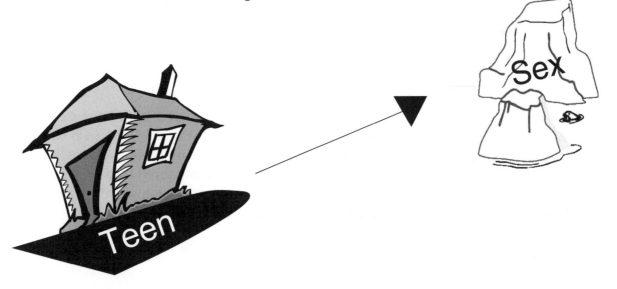

In the space provide below, list all that you have done in regards to your child's sexual behavior. Include conversations with this child about sex, books you have read, monitoring TV and music, curfews ... etc

_____

_____

_____

_____

_____

_____

_____

_____

_____

_____

_____

_____

_____

_____

_____

If the previous page is mostly blank, you are not alone. Many American parents have abdicated the responsibility of nurturing their child's sexual worldview to school, government, and media. **The results of this parental abdication have been disastrous.**

You cannot escape the responsibility of tomorrow by evading it today.
–Abraham Lincoln

CHAPTER 2

You Are Not Helpless!

I f the first step is understanding that you have a problem, the second step is understanding that you can influence the outcome of that problem. Yes, you matter. All parents matter in the lives of their children. And . . . are you ready for this? You can influence the decisions that they make when they are not around you. You can even influence the way they think about sex and when they think it is appropriate.

You won't use what you think you don't have.

This may sound like a given, but many parents don't believe they influence the way their children think about moral issues. If you don't believe that you have power over the way your children think, you will not exercise that power. Simply put, you won't use what you think you don't have. Perhaps you are suffering from what I call "Parental Learned Helplessness." A physiologist, B.F. Skinner coined Learned Helplessness in 1956. In my work as a public speaker, schoolteacher, youth leader and counselor, I come across what I call "Parental" Learned Helplessness almost daily. Let me explain classical "Learned Helplessness" before we move on to Parental Learned Helplessness. Skinner put a dog in a box divided in two by a partition. He had wires run to a steel sheet on the floor of each partition. He had the dog placed in one half of the partition.

He then sent an electric current into the sheet and shocked the dog. The dog, of coarse, jumped over the partition to the other compartment. Jumping out of the box was not an option for the dog. He would then shock the dog while it was sitting (quite relaxed) in the second compartment. The dog would jump back to the first compartment. (I think Skinner wasn't quite right.) He would then continue to shock the dog and the dog would continue to jump back and forth to avoid being shocked. Then something quite disturbing (and pitiful) would happen. The dog would stop jumping to the other compartment to avoid the shock. The dog would simply lie in one half of the compartment and allow himself to be shocked at predictable intravels. Even when Skinner turned off the electricity to the other half and tried to coax the dog over to it, the dog would not move. The dog had learned to be helpless. It had learned to be powerless. It had given up hope.

What then is Parental Learned Helplessness?

Parental Learned Helplessness - (PLH, pronounced Pla) - A feeling or attitude within the parent or parents that they have little or no influence over their child, often accompanied by a feeling of being overwhelmed by popular media and popular culture. P.L.H can be brought about by a past failure not even related to the child (i.e. divorce), or parental learned helplessness can set in after a series of battles perceived to have been lost by the parent (i.e. clothing, music). The parent then extrapolates a greater negative result out of a minor current event (i.e. my child talks back to me, therefore I don't matter, therefore he/she is going to have sex). Parent then gives up and assumes a defensive stance usually surrendering the remote control, the car keys and the home and barricades themselves in their bedroom.

Do you have symptoms of parental learned helplessness? Have you ever felt like giving up on lofty issues like virginity, morality, and honesty? Have you taken a "best I can do stance"? Keeping them clothed and fed is the "best I can do." Getting them to school and to their events is the "best I can do." Whether they graduate high school virgins or not is out of my hands! It's up to them to develop their own ideas of right and wrong. You're right. It is up to them to develop their own ideas of right and wrong, **after** they leave your home. While they are in your home it is your responsibility to help and guide the formation of those ideas.

I'm shocked . . . I can't believe you are watching that kind of stuff . . . and on my TV . . .

If you have an attitude of learned helplessness, you must defeat it. You must overcome the mindset that you are powerless or have little influence over your children's thoughts. Where did you get this idea? Does it come from your past or your own childhood relationship with your parents? Do you think such thoughts as, "I had sex when I was a teenager, so they are bound to have sex" or "I couldn't get their father to stay with me, how am I going to control them" or "I struggle to be a good parent on simple things like table manners, how am I going to implement such difficult concepts like right and wrong?"

Take time to list what you think is the reason for your P.L.H, Parental Learned Helplessness.

Then turn the page.

_____

_____

_____

_____

_____

_____

_____

_____

_____

_____

_____

_____

_____

_____

_____

okay . . . now turn the page

Read the next page and . . .
when it tells you to tear out this page . . .
tear it out

THAT WAS THEN, THIS IS NOW

I can guarantee one thing about everything that you've written on the proceeding page: it has all happened in the past. It doesn't matter why you don't think you can have a strong influence on your child's sexual behavior.

Your perceptions of your abilities as a parent have to do with the past.

It doesn't matter if you wrote down what you did as a child, your failed marriage, or your failure to get your children to clean their rooms yesterday.

Parental Learned Helplessness comes from your past not your future as a parent. Whatever is on the preceding page does not matter any more. You can change! You can change the way you parent. You can influence the way your children think. And you can definately influence the way they think about sex.

Tear out the preceding page (pages 11/12) and throw it away. Your past does not control your future. Your past as a parent does not control your future as a parent.

You are not helpless in the face of popular culture!

You matter!

Even if you feel overwhelmed now, you can still affect the behavior of the people around you. You can fight the garbage that threatens your family.

There is abundant evidence that you matter to the life of your children. In survey after survey the majority of children polled cited their parent(s) as the biggest influence on their life. Let me say this again. When polled, teenagers consistently state that parents have a large influence on their decision-making. It only **feels** like they are not listening!

78% of teenagers surveyed acknowledged that their parents had a lot of impact on their thoughts and deeds.[1]

Parents do have a powerful influence over their teen's sexual behavior if they have a loving relationship and <u>communicate their expectations</u> for the teen to practice abstinence. When teens have loving parents who encourage abstinence and not contraception, they are <u>twelve and a half times more likely to stay a virgin than</u> <u>those teens who have not heard these things from their parents.</u>[2]

78% of teens say they turn to parents in times of need. Interestingly, boys are more likely than girls to turn to their parents for advice (84 percent vs. 72 percent.) [3]

When adolescents were asked from whom they wanted to receive sexuality information, nearly all preferred their parents. [4]

"We're looking to you, the adults, to see how you respond to situations," said Laura Williams, a member of the Class of 2002 at Winnetonka High School in Kansas City, "and that's how we're going to make our decisions." [5]

You matter to your children!

They are watching your every move and recording every word and tone in their subconscious. Just because they don't do what you want them to do doesn't mean they haven't heard what you said. Go to the Reproducible Chapter and cut out figure R.1. Place figure R .1 next to your bathroom mirror. Believe it. Throughout this book I will direct you to the Reproducible Chapter in the back of the book. In that chapter you will find items you can copy (reproduce). Do it. I designed this book to be used, not simply read.

They only stop hearing you when you've stopped saying things and retreated to your bedroom, the office or the golf course.

CHAPTER 3

You're The Parent, Not A Friend

There exists yet another parent malady that we must address before we move onto specific strategies. You want to know what to "do" to your child but you won't do the things you need to do if you have this disease. I call this one the "Peace In Our Time" disease or P.I.O.T pronounced POT.

You must give up pot.

I'll explain. Here we go with one of my wacky analogies. Stay with me. It will make sense.

In 1938 Adolf Hitler was menacing all of Europe. The free world did not know what to do in the face of such a maniacal tyrant. Many countries argued for war against Hitler. But the Prime Minister of Britain, Neville Chamberlain, urged for peace. Hitler wanted Czechoslovakia. Chamberlain sought to appease Hitler and avoid war by allowing Germany to occupy Czechoslovakia. Hitler promised that he would stop aggression if allowed to take what he wanted.

In the Munich pact, signed also by France, Chamberlain accepted Hitler's territorial claims to predominantly German areas of Czechoslovakia. Chamberlain came home triumphant and proclaimed that his concession had brought "Peace In Our time."

You know the rest of the story. Hitler used the time he gained to grow stronger and attacked Poland in 1939. Chamberlain found himself at war with a bigger stronger Germany one year after he claimed to have bought peace. Think of all the suffering and misery that could have been avoided if Britain and France had stopped Germany early. Are you doing everything possible to avoid suffering and misery in your home?

We see that Chamberlain's goals appear to be lofty. He wanted "Peace In Our Time." Lets take a closer look at why this formula led to global disaster. Chamberlain was preoccupied with peace. Perhaps we should say that he wanted peace at all cost or P.A.C. No matter what you call it, it's clear that the evil brewing in Germany should have been confronted earlier. The other part of the formula is what led to disaster. He wanted peace, but only in our time. In other words he wanted peace now. It seems that he was preoccupied with having peace in the short term. I see this same disaster played out time and time again on a smaller scale.

All across America parents want peace. They want it now. They make concessions to get peace. They get it...for a while. Then they find themselves in a war.

Parents give up on curfews, fall back with expectations, and allow bad behavior, all to maintain family peace. The tired parent walks through the door and is confronted with foul language, bad TV choices, unmet responsibilities or any number of small infractions. The parent must make a choice. Do they confront, correct, and punish or do they let it slide? *It's just a small infraction. That catalogue isn't really pornography. That music is, after all, only music. Everybody swears. I'm tired. I want to relax. It's not worth fighting about. I'll just make a protest or two, maybe talk to him, and let it slide.* Many parents opt for immediate peace and find themselves at war years later. What does this have to do with you child's sexual behavior during his teen years? Everything.

Maybe if I make a face,
call them a name,
or make them feel guilty
they will let me get my way

If you choose short-term peace you may reap long-term war. If your seventh grade daughter flaunts her cleavage, listens to whatever she wants to, watches whatever she wants to, and doesn't allow you any input on her behavior, then what leads you to believe she won't stay out overnight and "shack up" when she is a sophomore?

Your quest to influence your child's sexual decision making will lead to conflict. How are you going to handle it?

If your thirteen year old son talks back, stays out past curfew, watches pornography with his friends, has his own pornography stash, and in general, doesn't respect any of the guidelines you set up, what makes you think he will respect your belief that he should wait? If he doesn't recognize any behavioral guidelines what makes you think he will recognize sexual guidelines? If he proclaims his freedom to view "adult" movies and material, what makes you think he will stop when given the opportunity to participate in the real thing?

You must understand that you should give up peace and engage in some short-term battles in order to produce a teenager who can make the right decisions about sex. A child who is a little off in his decision making in sixth grade will be way off in tenth (the average age for sexual intercourse). A child who does not suffer any consequences for bad decision-making in fifth grade will believe that nothing bad will happen to him for his actions in tenth.

What I'm saying is that conflict, for the right issues, is a good thing. Protracted peace, at all costs, is a bad thing.

If you have not been doing the right thing then when you start, get braced for conflict.

If your teenager doesn't hate you some of the time, somthing is wrong.

Why have parents allowed themselves to believe that if their child is unhappy or mad at them they've failed? Your teenager should be unhappy and mad at you some of the time; it's their job.

Your teenager may break the family peace when you set parameters. That's just too bad.

Your teenager may go to war when you start modifying his behavior and having input on the creation of his ideas about sex. That's too bad

You're the parent; you have a right to make your child unhappy. You're the parent; your child should be mad at you some of the time. You're the parent; you have a right to set limits and control behavior. You're the parent; it's your job to give up peace and enter into short-term war for the long term good of your child.

Repeat after me: **I'm the Parent**

Repeat after me: **I'm the Parent**

Repeat after me:
I'm Still A Good Parent If My Child Is Unhappy With Me

Appeasement parenting does not work. If you seek to appease your child you will lose his respect and your own. The strategies contained in this book will force you to abandon appeasement. Cut out Fig R.2 and R.3 and place prominently where you will see them every morning. Beside or on your bathroom mirror is ideal.

Don't wink at the small stuff or you will reap sorrow. Get bold, parents. Go to battle so that you will have long-term peace. Go to battle over small decisions so that big decisions (like whether or not to be sexually involved) fall in the right column.

Remember that you are the parent!

WARNING, THE ADVICE CONTAINED
IN THE REST OF THIS BOOK
IS BOUND TO CAUSE
SOME TEMPORARY FAMILY CONFLICT.
HANDLE AND IMPLEMENT WITH CARE.
WHEN FEELING FAINT OF HEART REREAD
CHAPTER THREE AND REPEAT, "I AM THE
PARENT" SEVERAL TIMES DAILY.

WE WILL PROGRESS
FROM EASIER TO
MORE DIFFICULT STRATIEIES.
EACH PROGRESSIVE CHAPTER
WILL REQUIRE MORE TIME
AND EMOTIONAL INVESTMENT
TO IMPLEMENT.

PART TWO

Strategies

Being a parent is tough. If you want a wonderful little creature to love, you can get a puppy.
– Barbara Walters

Liberty must be limited in order to be possessed.
– Edmund Burke

CHAPTER 4

Get In Their Social Life

When I was a teenager, if I pulled up to a girl's house, tooted the horn and she skipped out and got in the car, I was excited. I knew that I didn't really have to have her home at curfew. Now if, on the other hand, a big hairy arm stuck out the door and motioned for me to come in. And if the owner of that arm sat me down in his living room and made me uncomfortable in a friendly sort of way. And if he asked me where I was going with his daughter, whom he loves, and where were we going after the movie, and what was my home phone number? If the father did all those things EACH time I picked up his daughter. Do you think I had her home in time? Yes. Do you think I made a move on her? I don't think so.

**"Come on in . . .
I want to ask you
a few questions . . ."**

It amazes me that parents don't understand the importance of monitoring their child's social life. Oh they're worried, but for some reason they're reluctant to interfere.

**A parent should know the who, what, where, and when of their
teenager's life outside the home.**

One of the easiest ways to do that is at the pickup and drop off. Don't let this happen without you being there. When a young man shows up to take out your daughter, you need to put him through "the wringer." Put a hand on his shoulder, invite him in, sit him down in your den and ask him what his favorite football team is. Stand or sit close to him, just a little in his physical space. Have your spouse meet him. Get his cell and home phone number. Get the itinerary for their date. If they are just going to "hang out," that's fine. When and where are they going to be "hanging out?" Let this guy know that he has somebody to be accountable to. It's not just a girl; it's *your* girl. Keep him in that seat until you can see beads of sweat break out in his hairline. Then walk him to the door, remind him of when you expect to see your daughter again, give him a rather firm slap on the back, and tell him to have a nice evening.

Now, why do all this? Especially when you will be as uncomfortable as he is. Simple. You're making a statement to both him and your daughter. (Who will be mortified; see chapter three) It's not what comes out of your mouth that is so important. It's the gesture itself that has impact. By taking time out of your day and putting down the TV remote to go through this ritual you're saying, "What happens during this date matters to me." You're saying, "My daughter is very important to me." You're saying, "I now know who you are and I will hold you accountable for what happens this evening." And you're saying, "don't have sex."

Now you're thinking, "How could fifteen minutes in my living room say all that?" It will. The message will be there. He will get the message. He'll feel it when you give him a slap on the shoulder as he heads out the door. He'll hear it in your voice. He may not listen. But he will recognize that a shot has been fired across his bow.

I have found that many parents do go through this dance whenever their daughter interacts with a different boy. But they don't do it continuously with the *same* boy. Big mistake. You put the boy (or girl, we'll get to that later) through the wringer every time he shows up. Whether it's the first time he has been in your daughters life, or the twenty-third date. You get it so imprinted in this boy's mind that he has to account to you that he will come looking for you before he even thinks about pulling out of the driveway.

He pulls up and sees you in the backyard trimming hedges; well, he'll shuffle back there and bag the clippings. He will start telling you his plans for the afternoon before you ask. He knows the questions so he will give you the answers. What if he's lying? What if everything he tells you isn't true? It doesn't matter.

You can't control what he does. You can only have input.
It's your job to have as much input as possible.

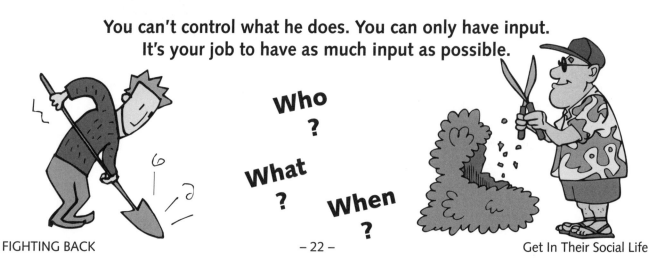

Who
?
What
?
When
?

What if there is no Dad in the house. Well, the woman of the house will have to put the boy through the "wringer." Ladies, you just invite him in, sit him down, pleasantly get in his face, and ask him all the same questions. And you do it each time he comes over.

Your daughter will hate you for the effort. (See chapter 3) If you have not been doing this from the start, she will protest. She will use all of her teenage manipulative tricks to get you to stop. She will probably be cold and sullen for three to four days. Of course, many of you have teens who are cold and sullen all the time. Her favorite line will be, "Nobody does that anymore!"

Well, she may be partially right. Understand, the children somehow obtain a manual when they turn thirteen.

The manual gives guidelines such as, "don't recognize your parents when you see them in the mall. Tell your parents "nobody else's parents do that... insult your parent's clothing, etc."

- Ignore them in public places
- Make fun of their clothing
- Do everything to make them feel ineffective
- Use selective hearing

You will be told that what you are doing is wrong and none of her/his friend's parents monitor their behavior and who they "hang out" with. Don't listen to them. It's in the manual. You're the parent. You can be their buddy when they grow up and are paying their own bills.

What about girls? Everything stays the same, just the roles change. That's right, you should put girls through the wringer. This is the new millennium. Girls can and will be just as sexually aggressive as guys. Girls who come into your son's life need to know where you stand on sexual issues. Now it's Mom's turn to take center stage. Mom, when that girl enters your home, you put your hand on her shoulder and tell her just how much you love your little boy.

Ask her what her plans are for the evening. Go over who, what, where, and when. Invite her into your kitchen, have her help out for a few minutes. Refer to your son as "my boy" or "our boy." Let her know that her little "hottie" has a home and people who love him. Develop a relationship.

Parents, move from intimidation to "dictatorial familiarity." You need to get familiar with your child's peer group, and also to be in control. You are going to move to authoritarian familiarity. You are going to become a familiar dictator. You start off as Stalin and then you morph into a cross between General Patton and Mr. Rodgers. I want you to build a relationship but continue to maintain your position of authority.

I want you to get to know the group as they continue to pass through your child's life. But do not try to become "in," "hip" or "cool." When you start this, "Get in their social life," step, you will be an intimidating figure. And you should be. But intimidation doesn't last as long as respect does. Am I asking you to get personal with your child's peer group? Precisely. You see, fear isn't as powerful as respect. Fear is immediate; respect is something that you will build over time. Because, remember, you are always there at the pickup and drop off.

I'm not asking you to make friends with your daughter's peer group. I'm asking you to get to know them. It's important that they know that you know them. And more importantly, that they know that you know that they know you have put an effort into knowing them. Got it?

Why do you want to build a relationship with some punk that is taking out your daughter? Why should you build an adult to teen relationship with your child's peer group? There are too many good reasons to list. But, let's try a few.

When you intimidate you are a force, and that's good in the beginning, it also takes less time to become a force. But you can't stay a force for long. You must move on to something more intimate. You must become a person. You see, over time, as this young man continues to show up on your doorstep, he will begin to understand that you have placed on him a series of expectations. He may meet those expectations out of fear, for awhile. But if you become an actual person in this boy's mind, then he may meet those expectations out of a desire to please you or at best not to disappoint you. (Of course, keeping a little of the fear element around doesn't hurt.)

In the beginning you want him/her to know that you will be upset if sexual activity ensues. Then you want him to know *why* you would be upset. For him to know why you would be upset he needs to get a glimpse of your value system. Don't misunderstand me; I'm not encouraging you to be buddy-buddy with your teen's peer group. I'm asking you to develop a presence in their minds. You want to matter. Intimidate, then communicate your value system and expectations.

Be a familiar dictator. You dictate the freedom he/she has with your daughter/son. You dictate how relaxed he can be with the relationship between you.

You're a very interested dictator and a benevolent one. You are the parent of your child and by default you are in an authoritative position over anyone who comes into your home.

The other reason to get to know the boy or the girl your child is dating or hanging around with is that it's the right thing to do.

What has led you to believe that you are *not supposed* to be "minding their business?"

You *are* supposed to be minding their business. You're the parent, and it's what you do. Hands off parenting has produced the headlines we have today. Am I advocating a totalitarian regime? Not exactly, I'm advocating a *loving* totalitarian regime.

Do you need to know whom your children are hanging out with, where they are going and when they should be expected back? Yes!

You can't release what you never held. You can't gradually lift restrictions if you never put restrictions in place. Eventually, your children will leave the home. That is when you will have to restrict yourself and "stop minding their business," unless you are paying for college or supporting them any other way. But the idea that you are being intrusive when you want to know exactly what your fifteen year old is doing is ludicrous.

What about the new dating? Here's the Old and New Word descriptions . . .

Old Word	New Word
Date	Hang out, chill, see, meet, get together, meet some friends, all going, group thing,
Boyfriend/girlfriend	Friend, homey, buddy, homeboy
Sex, made out	Hooked up, freaky, too many to list

I was once speaking with the mother of a girl I taught when I was a schoolteacher. We got on the topic of teen pregnancy. The mother declared, "I don't have to worry about that. Joan doesn't date and doesn't have a boyfriend." I was exasperated because I knew that Joan was very active with boys and had been involved with several relationships.

Don't look for the vocabulary that we used growing up. You will most likely never hear it. Your child will never come home and say that she is going on a "date" with her "boyfriend." So, if you are waiting for your children to start "dating" before you step in then you are making a mistake. He/she probably already is dating and you have not recognized it as such because you are looking for the old vocabulary and behavior pattern. You remember how it was done. The guy would have to initiate. He would pick somebody he liked, work up the nerve and then ask her. Then they would go to a specific event or place (already predetermined and approved by her) for their "date."

Often, they don't date, they "hang out." Kids today are much more ambiguous. If you're looking for old patterns you may wait awhile. They don't always date like we did. They do this "group" thing. A car pulls up with some guys and girls in it and your son runs out and jumps in. You ask him what they are going to do that night and he shouts, "Hangout" as he runs across the yard. You call him over and motion to the car, "Which one is your girlfriend?" you ask. He just looks at you like you're stupid, "None" he replies. You contentedly go back to your yard work, happy that your son isn't dating yet. Guess what, he's dating. Guess what, he could be sexually active with one of the girls he's "not dating." Don't fall asleep at the wheel while you're on the road. I hear, "When my son/daughter starts dating I'll get more involved". I hear it so often that I want to scream, "Just because they are not 'dating' doesn't mean they aren't having sex!"

You need to redefine when your son or daughter is at risk for sexual activity.

Your son or daughter is at risk for sexual activity if they are with a member of the opposite sex, either in a group or one-on-one setting, outside of adult supervision for more than one second.

Stop looking for dating the way you did it, and start monitoring their social life as if they're on a "date" every time they go out the door.

Oh, okay . . . maybe I should start monitoring their social life . . .

Think, "I will monitor their social life." Not, "I will monitor their dating life."

How do you deal with this "new dating?" Just modify your tactics. Kids tend to run in groups or tribes. They will also have sex within this tribe. They don't date individuals they date a tribe. They hang out in coed groups. When the tribe shows up to pick up your daughter or son put the whole tribe through the wringer. That's it. Instead of asking whom, what, when, and where, from an individual, you address the tribe.

The tribe has a collective conscience. You let that collective conscience know how you feel about the time that your child will be out of your sight.

It's your job to "track the tribe." That's right, you need to know something about your child's primary social group. Who are these guys and gals that Jr. is hanging out with? What are their phone numbers? Where do they live? Who are their parents? How are they doing in school?

How do you put the tribe through the wringer? The same way you put an individual through the wringer. You get face-to-face contact time.

A mini van pulls into your driveway with five kids in it. If they don't come in then you send your teenager out with the absolutely horrific, repulsive, and degrading task of telling them they have to come in for a second to say "Hi" to mom/dad or both.

You insist on this. Now if you haven't been doing this, then prepare for the first battle brought about by this book. (If you fight with your child for six months after bringing home this book, you are on the right track.)

Tell your child squarely, "You can't leave tonight unless they get out of the vehicle and spend some time with me." Now, you can meet with them in the driveway or on the front step. Remember that everyone gets out of the car. It's a control thing. You're in control. Don't be as aggressive with the tribe as you are with one individual of the opposite sex. If you see a new member in the crowd, get contact info.

What are you saying with this gross violation of teenage culture? You're saying, "I know who my daughter/son is with. I've looked you in the eyes. You know this sweetie has a real mother/father. I know where you're going, I will be here at the drop off."

We'll see you at the drop off!

You say all this with your actions. The tribe will be a little shell-shocked when you first do this. They will stand around your foyer looking like lemmings searching for a cliff to jump off.

Remember to casually mention that you'll be seeing them at the drop off. Something like, "Well, you can tell me about the movie when you swing by."

Try to make this as bearable as possible for the tribe. Think of yourself as a kind dentist trying to extract a tooth. Do what you have to do, but be as respectful about it as possible. Try to put the tribe in a comfortable position as you put them through the wringer. You can spend most of the time talking about the prospects for the school football team or what they think of Jenny Lo. Getting the info you want doesn't have to be the whole conversation, just part of it. Remember, you're a *benevolent* dictator.

You get face time or the hostage doesn't leave the building.

After putting the tribe through the wringer for the first time your teenager may protest, "My friends won't pick me up because you bugged them last week." First of all, they probably *will* pick him or her up. Jr. is just being dramatic hoping you will be intimidated and won't stage a repeat performance. But it could be quite possible that your kid's being left out because you insisted on getting some face time with the tribe. Let me ask you a question. What does it tell you about the group that your teen is running with if they won't tolerate the slightest scrutiny? You're only asking for five minutes. You did it in a nice way. The only direct question you asked was "What are you doing tonight?"

One thing to remember about this ritual is to make it a ritual, conistency is key. That's right: **You employ "the wringer" every time an individual or a group shows up to pick up your child. You get the wringer out if your son or daughter is leaving. If four guys show up to pick up your son or three girls to pick up your daughter, if the departing group is coed or not, if they drive over or walk over: you get face time or the hostage doesn't leave the building.**

This is important. You make monitoring your child's social life a constant. What's nice about this is anything you make a constant becomes easier. If you stick to your guns this will become a *habit* for everyone involved. One afternoon you'll open the front door and there will be the whole tribe. Your daughter won't have to go out and invite them in; they will just do it. They'll come in, use the bathroom, get something to eat, and answer your questions. Some of them will even like it. That's right some members of the tribe will like your attention. They may have no contact with *their* parents, but at least they know somebody cares about them.

Don't Stop Being In Their Business!

REMEMBER You're The Parent

You may be thinking, "None of this is my business and is all this really necessary?" Now there you go with that 70's garbage again. Didn't I talk to you about this? Hands off parenting hasn't worked. Letting them "explore themselves" has led to a youth culture adrift. You're the parent! You have a right to know about the people your teenager is spending time with. You have this right until your child turns eighteen and moves out. And if they don't move out after they are eighteen then you still have this right because they are under your roof. Cut out and post Figure R-4.

The Reverse Wringer

If only life were so simple that all your child's social outings started at your home. But they don't. They go from school to football games. You drop them off. They go from practice to a friends or from friends to a civic event. In these type situations you apply the wringer in reverse. You get all the facts from your child or you get all the facts from the tribe or individual at the other destination.

Let's go with the daughter/tribe transaction. You pull up to a house and your daughter is about to skip out and go up the front walk to meet the tribe at her destination (a member of the tribe's house). You get out and go to the door, or you tell your child to have a parent wave from the door. Reverse the wringer. Now you won't have to do any of this if you have the correct number for her destination. You could simply call and talk to Mom. You have phone numbers for all your daughter's friends don't you? You have numbers for all your son's buddies don't you? You have the numbers for all their favorite hangouts, don't you? I thought so.

**The point is that you can apply the wringer
wherever Teen Transactions (TnT) takes place.**

**If you can't apply it personally then you can apply it over the phone.
If you have the numbers, all the numbers . . .**

The Tribe Tracker

Find the Tribe Tracker (R.5). This contact sheet is a tool you will use for the rest of your teen's teen years.   We will talk about it here and then you will follow the instructions across from the form when you sit down with your teen and fill it out. Before you fill it out run it off. Don't be lazy, run it off at the copy store. You may need more than one sheet to track the tribe or you may loose it or your teenager may burn it. Please follow the directions and fill out the Tribe Tracker (R5)

Keep in mind your child will resist. It's their job. It is not an unreasonable request to want to know contact information. However, if you have previously bought into the parent as a buddy lie, then it will be a hard sell. Why do you want this information? Because you love them. You must put effort into monitoring their lives while they are out of your presence and you should have information on the people they are with. Many American parents are disconnected from their children's "outside" life. For many families, this disconnection has led to disaster.

Asking whom, what, where, and when from your child and the tribe is not intrusive. You're being a good parent when you gather information on your teen's activities outside your home.

You're being "intrusive" when you tell your twenty-five year old who to hang out with or how to change a diaper.

What about the non-dating movement?

As abstinence and virginity become more and more popular or "cool" new teen trends are emerging. There is a sub culture in teen behavior that I will call the "non dating movement," for lack of a better term. This movement is made up of teens that have decided to forgo dating until they are looking for a lifetime mate. The philosophy behind this movement is most easily stated as, "why go shopping if you're not ready to buy?"

One last nag . . .

Need more motivation to be vigilant about your teen's social life?
Consider this statistical picture of American youth. Every day in America:

- 1,000 unwed teenage girls become mothers
- 1,106 teenage girls get abortions
- 4,219 teenagers contract sexually transmitted diseases

- 500 adolescents begin using drugs
- 1,000 adolescents begin drinking alcohol
- 135,000 kids bring guns or other weapons to school
- 3,610 teens are assaulted; 80 are raped
- 2,200 teens drop out of high school
- 6 teens commit suicide[1]

Take a look at the above. All these events have something in common. They are all most likely to take place outside of direct parental supervision. And all of these behaviors except for the last two are social behaviors.

"Action Plan" Instructions

After each chapter in section two you will be asked to file an "Action Plan." Reading this book is a waste of your time unless you take action on the information it contains. Each chapter should elicit a series of responses while you read. You will think, "Oh, I need to do that," or, "I could do that but not the way described, maybe a little different." Or, "I need to pick up that book by the end of the week." If you don't write down these thoughts and ideas they are less likely to happen. Writing down and placing a date next to a task is a powerful thing. Doing it with your spouse is more powerful. Take the time to fill out each "Action Plan."

Transfer any dated goals to your palm pilot, planner or calendar. That way you will actually do them.

Action Plan

As a result of reading this chapter what are you going to do and when are you going to do it?

Examples - *We will fill out the tribe tracker with Jennifer on Saturday afternoon.*

I will start asking Joey to bring friends in before he heads out. I'm going to tell him that I will be doing this on Thursday.

This weekend Bill and I will take turns being the one who waits up to do the greeting and inspection when our daughter returns from any social outing, whether it's called a date or not.

_____

_____

_____

_____

_____

_____

_____

_____

_____

_____

_____

CHAPTER 5

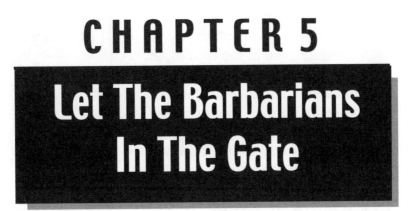

Let The Barbarians In The Gate

Studies have shown that sometimes teens have sex simply because it was "too easy" or they had "run out of things to do." Sex happens. One place and time that sex won't happen is in your home when you're there. This seems like a no brainer, but many parents are missing out on this one. It is a no brainer.

Your kids (or any one else's) won't have sex in your house if you're in the house.

You can worry about them while they're out cruising Main Street or you cannot worry about them while they tear up your den. It's up to you.

Teenagers are going to hang out, they are going to socialize, and they are going to develop relationships with the opposite sex. This is healthy. Your goal is not to stop the contact. Your goal is to control the when and where and to instill a value system that ensures that no harm is done while socializing. One of the ways you can do that is to open up your home to "the tribe". That's right; let the barbarians in the gate.

Let the barbarians in the gate.

Teenagers run out of things to do and places to go on a Friday night. Now, never mind that there is plenty to do and see. In their minds they run out of options right after they get out of the movie. They all meet at McDonalds and they get kicked out of there. Then they go to the pizza joint and get run out of there. They want a place to gather so they park at the Wal-Mart parking lot until the cops chase them off. What they want more than the movies or food or putt putt golf is a place to hang out and talk. As you know, they love to talk. Not necessarily to you (we'll work on that later) but to each other.

What all the options lack is simply a place for teens to gather and talk without having to buy something, ride something, or eat something. This desire will lead them to some unsupervised location. They will find a place to park where they won't get runoff. Or they will find a home where the parents are not. This home can be a member of the tribe's parents. That member of the tribe makes it known that his parents are out overnight and the tribe shows up. Kids show up because they want to socialize, talk, and be seen; but because there is no adult in the house, sex happens. They have sex for many reasons: one of them is because they can. They have ended up in a place, and I'm talking about a physical place, where sex for them is possible. There is no adult supervision, like at the movies, at McDonalds, at the pizza joint or at the mall. No, the manager at McDonalds was not supervising your child as closely as you would, but he would not allow him to disrobe. What I'm getting at is that your teenager's desire to socialize and congregate unhindered by outside distraction will put him/her in a situation where sex is possible.

Their desire to socialize in groups may drive them to a location where sex is possible.

If your teen is emotionally strong and you have worked hard to instill a view of abstinence as desirable, and they feel loved and are confident of their place in the world they will not have sex.

If they know that their mommy and daddy love them and that they do not have to perform sexually to be worthy of love, then they will be ok. They will have developed strong internal guidance and they won't have sex. That's a lot of ifs.

If you are "behind" in helping to develop your child's sexual worldview, the above scenario, two teens alone in a house or car, is bad. Now, if you follow directions in the rest of this book you will get to a mental place where you know that you know that you know that your teen will not have sex no matter where they are and whether they are supervised or not. But you are not there yet and probably neither are they.

So, you need to give them a place to go after they get out of the movies/mall/putt-putt/pizza. Your house is it. "They never will come here," you're thinking. "My teenager wants to get as for away from me as possible." Yes they do. But you can use one teenage impulse to override another. They want a place to be them. Here's what you do. Write off a section of your house as the "tribe's room." You can write it off for Friday and Saturday night, the whole weekend or if the room is not critical, the whole week. Now discuss this as a married couple. You have to do this as a team.

There is one important thing about this room or area that you choose. You can't be in it when "they" are in it. They will never show up. You can't be in the next room through an open doorway either; they won't come back. If you are in the next room you need to be separated by a door that's open some of the time and closed some of the time. Don't worry, you're going to open it periodically. The point is that you need to be in the house but not in the same room. You're thinking, "Isn't that the same as letting them park down a dirt road?" No, because you are in the house. They know that you are in the house; you know that they are in the house, and they know that you know that they are in the house. This means that you can pop in at any time. Today's youth culture has not yet gotten so defiant that kids will initiate intercourse with you in and out of the room.

Now you explain to your son or daughter the new hang out situation. It sounds something like this:

YOU	Honey, if you and your friends want to hang out in the basement/den/garage/ porch tonight that's fine.
TFD	(Teenager Feigning Disinterest) from now on referred to as TFD (pronounced teft) - Aw mom, we don't want to do that.
YOU	Well if you run out of places to go or things to do you can stop by.
TFD	Oh.
YOU	Yeah, I'll have chips and sodas if you want to and Dad moved the old stereo into the basement.
TFD	Oh. What time do we have to come by?
YOU	Whatever time you want as long as it's before your curfew.
TFD	Oh.

Now, we know teenagers love food and music, and you've provided for that. Don't act too eager because teens are programmed to never do anything they sense you want them to do very badly. Just mention it casually once in awhile. I've never had a parent report that the tribe showed up at the home hangout the first night it was offered.   I would be surprised if it ever happens. If it does, e-mail me and I will include your testimony in the rewrite of this book. Trust me, if you meet the requirements listed below for a home hangout, they will eventually show up:

1. Hangout is a separate area of the home.

2. You make it a point not to be a fixture in same room as hangout (ex: you are in the kitchen and they are in the den.)

3. The hangout has a cd/tape player, darts, ping pong, etc.

4. The hangout has access to food and drink.

5. They can arrive at hangout any time they want as long as it's before curfew.

Now, just when you think it's not going to happen, they will show up. You will hear their car in the driveway and know that this is the night. Do not, under any circumstances, run to the door to greet the tribe; they will disappear. Do not appear to them within the first ten minutes; they will become spooked and flee to the abandoned parking lots and dirt roads. You can make your first "pop" about thirty minutes after they arrive. You just "pop" into their room to say hello and make sure they have enough food, maybe some small chat and then leave. What you're saying is "I'm here and I know you're here. I'll be popping in and out as the evening progresses so: no smoking, no drinking, no swearing and no sex." They will resent the popping. They're teenagers, and it's their job to resent any supervision. They will resent it ... but they'll stay because they have a place to be them.

It helps if you can find a cheap ping-pong table or pool table. This is a real draw. I once met a dad who made the supreme sacrifice. He showed me a photograph of his workshop. It was a man's dream garage. He had tools hanging neatly on the wall and a rebuilt Chevy Chevell parked in the center, as if expecting worship. He then showed me another picture of the same space. The tools were boxed up and the automotive implements that were not boxed were covered with sheets. And where the Chevell had been stood a ping-pong table. "A man's gotta do what a man's gotta do," he said with a grimace.

"If you build it they will come."

They will come. And when they do you have several ways to let them know what is expected and perhaps more importantly, what isn't expected. Just by being there you have let your guests know who you are, and that they are your guests. When you "popped" the first time you let them know that they are being monitored "from afar."

You can also set the tone for the room itself. Get your son or daughter in on the act. Help them feel like this room will be acceptd by the group. Put up teen themed decorations. Order some of the abstinence promoting posters and signage from the Abstinence Clearinghouse (Listed in resource section) Remember, this is their room. You are not supposed to like the way it looks. Let them pick some of "their" posters as long as they don't promote dangerous behaviors. The gang will pick up on it even though they don't acknowledge it.

Before we go any futher I need to let you know I'm not advocating the newest stupid parent trick (STP pronounced, stip): the coed sleep over. None of these people are staying over and none should show up with a sleeping bag and a toothbrush. There should not be any sleeping equipment in the hang out room. As far as "coed sleepovers," all I have to say to those *hip* and *in* parents is, "what were you thinking?"

Announce some rules. Of course any mention of rules and they will disappear so don't call them rules. Don't call them anything. Maybe after your second "pop," (Did I mention that you would be popping throughout the night?) you can make a little remark or joke. You lean in to throw in a bag of potato chips and comment, "Remember, no smoking swearing or making out."

And you're gone. Don't lecture, don't extrapolate, and don't even wait for them to acknowledge that they heard. Just get it out as quick as you can and be gone. Remember, it's the first night and you don't want to scare them off. You don't want them to smoke, swear and make out but you don't want to be so parental that you scare them off to a place where they *can* smoke, swear and hang out.

Now you have declared what is important to you. Go back up to your bedroom, watch TV, make love to your spouse (remember you're legal) whatever, just don't go back in "their room" for at least a half-hour. Now you have set the minimum guidelines and, for them, they may be a struggle to meet. Don't add any more rules but the basics. They will crank the stereo real loud. When they first get in they will crank it extremely loud just to see if they can make you reappear. When their ears start to hurt they will lower it.

Now, the first time they show up the tribe will send a scouting party. It may just be your child and one other friend. Soon there will be more. When you get two or more boys in the group you will begin to hear the thumping and crashing I described above. Don't be alarmed, boys push and shove when gathered in groups with girls present. It's what they do.

You will hear stuff crash and bodies thump against the wall. Just hunker down until it is your time to "pop." Now, this group may actually grow. You have to decide if you want to provide a safe place for your child and his/her close friends or do a teen outreach kind of thing. Your "hangout" could remain four to six kids or grow to twenty. It's up to you and your children how far you want to go with this.

Every teen that walks into your home should be made aware of the three rules, as subtlely as possible, but it has to be done. Every teen that walks into your home should go into your Tribe Tracker (see chapter four). Now if your group gets above ten you may want to post the rules. See Fig R.6 in Reproducible Chapter. Copy the page in earth colors or whatever is the popular teen tone at the time of this reading.

The "hangout" also gives you a chance to do something very important: get to know your child's peer group and, get to know their parents. I'm often shocked when faced with an audience of parents. I always conduct some polls of my audience. I often ask the parents to raise their hand if they know the first and last names of their child's two best friends. I then ask them to raise their hand if those two children's phone numbers are in their palm pilot, or their organizer or posted near the phone. I then ask the few remaining parents what they know about this child's family. Are the parents married? Are they living together? Is there a gun in the house? Do they know where you stand on issues such as sex, drugs and alcohol? Do they have your phone number? Often, out of a crowd of hundreds of parents, only one or two hands remain up after I finish my questioning. Use the "hang out" as a time to get information. Kids will forget stuff. They will have things dropped off. Go out in the driveway and talk to parents of your child's friends. Your teens need to know that you have numbers and that you are comfortable talking to the tribe's parents. Invite them in. This will horrify your kids, but remember, its okay to horrify your kids. (See chapter three)

Don't worry; just work on getting them into your basement and aware that there is no touching, smoking, or swearing while they are there.

Will your teenagers actually stay home on Friday or Saturday night? Absolutely! I've heard of it happening and seen it with my own eyes.

We've spent a lot of time on this, but we did it for several reasons. When you open up your home you:

1. Provide a safe and somewhat monitored environment for your teen.

2. Demonstrate your love for your teen by putting time and energy into this effort and sacrificing a portion of your home.

3. Make a firm stand for abstinence. Your teen will sense that not having sex has to do with at least part of your decision and this effort.

4. Have an opportunity to get to know more members of "the tribe" and get phone numbers for them.

5. Create opportunities to meet parents of the tribe.

You have done more than open up your home. You have provided a "no sexual pressure zone" for your teen and the tribe.

You have provided a place where it is okay to be a virgin and get along with your parents. I'm talking about a physical place where they can feel physically safe. You have provided a sanctuary.

Action Plan

As a result of reading this chapter, what are you going to do and when are you going to do it?

Examples - *Hubby will clean out garage on ____/____/____*

We will tell Jr. our house is open. Then we will go out and get some cool stuff to put on the walls of the basement to make it his teen hangout room on ____/____/____

I will get rules copied and posted by this weekend

_____

_____

_____

_____

_____

_____

_____

_____

_____

_____

_____

_____

The best way to keep children home is to make
the home atmosphere pleasant – and to
let the air out of the tires.
– Dorothy Parker

We cannot solve life problems
except by solving them.
– M Scott Peck

CHAPTER 6

Curfews & Controlling the Window of Exposure

Curfews have created conflict between parents and teens forever. I choose to write about curfews separate from chapter three (monitoring their social life) because curfews should be applicable whether on a date or not, whether out with friends or out running errands on their own. You should always know when your child is returning and they should always know when they are expected to return. Every time your teen slams the front door or skips out the back there should be an agreed upon time they are expected home. Is it midday and your daughter is going out to lunch with a female member of the tribe. What time is she expected home? Is your son going out to the mall to check out sneakers? What time is he expected home? It amazes me that some parents let their kids waltz out the door on a Saturday morning and not have any idea when they will be back.

> A curfew is not just for nights.
> They should be used at any time. Think of curfews as brackets.
> Every time your teen is heading somewhere give him a bracket.
> The bracket indicates when he is free to go and
> when he/she is expected to return.

What does this have to do with sexual behavior? Surveys of teens have turned up some pretty disturbing trends. When asked why their first sexual encounter occurred, many teens answered, "Because we could." In other words, they found themselves in a situation where they were unmonitored and had enough time. Another answer that popped up often was, "We got bored" or "We ran out of things to do."

Many of you have tried the curfew battle and given up, or worse, allowed yourself to be pushed back. I know a parent has been beat on curfews when I run into something like this: a freshman that is able to stay out until 1:00 am on a Saturday night or an eighth grader that is up until 12:30 am on a Friday night. This is what I call "loss of curfew credibility" and it is tough to regain.

The reasons curfews are worth the battle are legion. Let's look at a few:

- By setting a beginning and ending time to your child's social adventures you are defining what a scientist would call the "widow of exposure." Stated as simply as possible - By controlling the beginning and ending of the social period you are limiting the time Jr. can get into trouble.

- By setting a beginning and ending time you know when you should appear to execute "the wringer." If you don't know exactly when your daughter is expected home, how can you greet her at the door?

- Setting curfews says "I love you" in a language your teenager understands, even if they won't admit it. Remember, discipline equals love.

- Kids need parameters. A curfew is a very real parameter.

- Curfews can be adjusted if the child does not meet your expectations in other areas. However, if you are not setting curfews or have lost your curfew credibility, you have nothing to negotiate with.

Curfews are *earned*. They do not come automatically with age or grade level. For example, telling your teen, "When you're in tenth grade you can stay out to eleven o'clock and when you are in eleventh you can stay out until twelve," is the wrong approach. A tenth grader that has bad grades, has been disrespectful to you, and has not shown the ability to make the positive choices that are expected of tenth graders, should not have the same curfew as a teenager that is doing all the above appropriately.

So then how should you set curfews? When doing workshops I am constantly surrounded by parents who ask, "My child is in tenth grade, what curfew should he have?" or, "My fifteen year old wants to stay out until eleven, what should I do?" or "My daughter wants to stay out with her boyfriend until twelve, is that ok?" I refuse to answer all such questions.

I don't know the child involved. Has he met his responsibilities? Does he even have responsibilities? What are his grades like? Is he involved with any organized activities outside of school? What is happening in the town you live in? How safe are the streets?

If you are having difficulty setting curfews then you may be going about it all wrong. You don't have to set curfews; your child can set and pick his own curfews. That's right, *they* set their own curfews. They pick what time they will be expected home by their actions. Stated simply, if your child meets your expectations he gets to stay out longer. If Jr. does not meet your expectation he is expected in earlier or he can't go out at all. Getting to stay out later isn't up to you, its up to your child, (within reason).

Curfews in your home should never be set based on grade level or age. The new marker is behavior . . . and, curfews are negotiated weekly. So after reading this chapter, and perhaps rereading Chapter 2, you meet with Jr. and have the following conversation.   This conversation was taped and reproduced for your benefit.

We will drop in as two parents try to regain control (because they *are* the parents), of their teen. The parents, Bob and Beth Milquetoast, have allowed their tenth grade boy, Bucky, to push his Friday and Saturday night curfew back to eleven oclock. Not only that, but they have also stopped requiring Bucky to give an itinerary for his social adventures. (They fell for the "Nobody does that" line.)

Bob and Beth are not happy with the music choices that Bucky is making, the pornography on his walls, or the web sites he has been caught visiting. They failed to connect his behavior to any consequences. They were vaguely aware that their son was at risk for sexual activity, and that late nights increased that risk. But hadn't taken any action.

Often, Bucky comes in at eleven thirty or twelve. He has excuses and Bob and Beth let him slide. They don't want conflict. But Bob and Beth have been through therapy and they are now involved with a parenting class. They are now going to set down the new curfew guidelines with Bucky:

This conversation takes place at the kitchen table. Bob and Beth are seated side by side in order to show unity.

Bob   Bucky will you come here for a moment? Your mother and I would like to speak with you.

Bucky   *(after waiting the appropriate time that all teenagers must wait when responding to a request.)* Ok.

Bob   Your mother and I have decided to change your curfew.

Bucky   *Now immediately interested.* Oh, what is it?

Beth   Well it's not really a set time anymore. *(Bucky perks up.)* From now on your curfew will depend on your behavior. *Bucky slumps.*

Bob   What time you get to stay out till will also depend on how well you are able to explain what you will be doing.

Bucky What are you talking about? *(He starts to get up.)*

Bob Sit down. *Bucky sits down slowly. He is not used to dealing with Mom and Dad at the same time. His preferred technique is to divide them. He is also not used to Dad backing up Mom. Inside he is freaking out but he maintains a calm exterior. On a very deep level, he is beginning to realize that a very fundamental shift in power has occurred right before his eyes.*

Beth Your base curfew on Friday and Saturday night is now ten o'clock.

Bucky Ten O'clock!

Bob Don't raise your voice to your mother.

Bucky Nobody else has to be in at ten. Joey's parents don't give him a curfew; he gets to stay out until he wants.

Bob We don't care what Joey's parents are doing. We are not Joey's parents.

Beth Ten o'clock is your base weekend curfew. It can be moved later or earlier based on your behavior and school performance for the previous week. It will also depend upon whom you are going out with and what you are doing.

Bucky That's too complicated.

Bob No, it's really quite simple.

Beth For every grade that you receive below a C on your progress report or report card you will lose two hours off your base time.

Bob For every chore that remains undone after a 24-hour period you will loose another hour.

Beth Each instance you raise your voice to your father or me you will lose one hour.

Bob If you skip a class you will lose one hour each. Unless you have worked something out with your mother or me previously, you will loose that hour.

Bob But you can gain time.

Beth That's right. If you make B honor roll on your card or interim report you will get a standing additional hour until the next card or interim comes out.

Bucky *Perking up* – You mean I could stay out to eleven.

Bob Yes. As long as you didn't mess up in other areas. For example, If you had one of your little fits twice that week you would lose two hours under the talk back rule. So you would have gained an hour because of your grades and lost two because of your behavior.

Bucky So it would be my base time, ten o'clock, plus one minus two. So I would have to come in at nine o'clock that weekend.

Beth For that particular weekend, yes.

Bob You can also gain time in another way. If you can tell us your exact itinerary while you're out, and we can check it by phone by talking to another parent or supervisor, you earn an hour.

Bucky What's itinerary mean?

Beth Where you are going to be and when you are going to be there?

Bob So let's say this Friday, when all is said and done, you have an earned curfew of ten o'clock. If you can tell us where you are going to be for the evening, especially from ten until eleven, you will get to stay out until eleven.

Bucky My old curfew time.

Bob *Ignoring the sarcasm* – So, let's say you can give me an hour by hour when and where with phone numbers, then you're good. And you have to be very specific with that additional hour. So, let's say you tell me that you are going to be watching videos in Joey's basement from ten o'clock until eleven, I had better be able to call his parents and confirm it. If I can't then you're grounded for one night the next weekend.

Bucky *Sits for a moment, taking it all in, then perks up.* – So, if I make B honor roll and I am able to give you an exact itinerary for the evening, and I do nothing wrong or disrespectful the whole week, I may be able to stay out until twelve Friday and Saturday night.

Beth That's right.

Bob As long as you are in a home with a parent or supervisor inside from ten o'clock to twelve.

Bob You must be able to give an exact and verifiable by phone location for the evening, especially for the additional two hours you earned past "base time."

Bucky Well you can call me on the cell.

Bob As long as you can hand your cell to somebody's parent or guardian if I ask you to.

Beth *(Placing her hand on Bob's knee.)* Remember Honey, there is one other thing.

Bob That's right. We'll call this the co-ed rule. If the group you are in is coed you must be at a verifiable location in hour increments during your whole outing.

Bucky *Who was showing signs of acceptance, starts motioning, flustered.* What do you mean all times? How can I know where we will be?

Bob Plan it.

Beth Ok, let's say it's a Friday night and you have earned the right to stay out until eleven o'clock. You get one hour past your base time so you would have had to account for that hour anyway. But since the group is co-ed you have to file a "flight plan" before you leave. So, you could tell us you are going to a movie with your friends at 8:30. You will get out of there around 10:00. You need to be able to tell us exactly where you will be from 10:00 until 11:00.

Bucky Are you guys going to call every place I say I'm going to be?

Bob No, we *may not* check on you all evening, then again, we may. But you see, you're really going to only be at two locations during the above example. So, we would only have to place one call. We aren't going to call the theater; we will have to trust you on that location. But, and it is important that you understand this. You must be at a reachable location any time you are out past your base time of 10:00.

Bucky *Face contorted into his best "persecuted teenager look"* – I can't believe this.

Bob If you raise your voice to us again, your mother and I will not get upset, however, you will lose one hour off your curfew time for this weekend.

Bucky *(Quickly settles down.)*

Bob So your base time is 10:00. If you fail to perform a chore or are disrespectful to a family member you will lose an hour for each incident. For any time that you earn past 10:00 you must be reachable and in a supervised location and we must be able to speak with a supervisor if we wish.

Beth Now, the coed rule comes into play whenever you are in a coed group. *Frowns at the obvious statement.* When the coed rule is in play you must give us an hour by hour itinerary for the evening.

Bob Once again, you must be reachable the whole evening when the coed rule is in affect.

Bucky *Facing a unified front, slumps in his chair.*

Bob Now if you handle yourself well, and you are responsible with your freedom...

Bucky What freedom, your monitoring my every move, I don't have any freedom.

Bob That's not accurate, no freedom would be you grounded and in your room.

Bucky *Staring at the floor and nodding in resignation, sighs barley audible* – Yeah.

Bob As I was saying. If you show yourself to be accountable, especially in a coed group, you may be able to move your base time back.

Bucky When can I move my base time back.

Bob Well, let's see how well you do with 10:00. The way you have been behaving, just earning ten and then eleven is going to be a challenge.

Beth Remember the form honey.

Bob *Reaches for a piece of paper and places it on the coffee table.* Just so we understand the way everything will be lets fill in and sign this form.

Bucky A form?

Beth Bucky this form works for you just as it does for us. Let's say that you earn the right to stay out until twelve and your Dad and I dispute it. You could get this form and show us what we agreed on.

Bob Look Bucky, your Mom and I don't want to do all this but we have to. If you can build some depth and character we wouldn't have to do this at all.

Narrator *Bucky and his parents fill out the form. Bucky spends the rest of the week trying to get his parents to cave in by being sullen and silent. But Bob and Beth don't cave in because their therapist has taught them that it is ok if their children are unhappy with them. They also do not allow Bucky to engage them in discussion about what was agreed upon at "the signing". They watch for indications that Bucky is trying to divide them. Their therapist has told them to watch for this.*

Do you see the beauty? You only set the base time. These parents had to set their base time at ten o'clock because Bucky had been staying out to eleven and eleven thirty no matter what his behavior the previous week. He also did not have to give an account of where he would be while he was out. This put them in a bad position. They had lost credibility and they are now going to have to fight to regain it. The important thing is that if Bucky finds himself with a curfew of, say, eight o'clock, he has no one to blame but himself.

Obviously, the above approach can be modified but there are four important features of this approach that you must not abandon.

1. The curfew is earned. It is not given by age or grade.
2. Time can also be earned if the child is able to account for his whereabouts and his whereabouts are verifiable.
3. If the group is coed he is required to meet a higher standard of accountability.
4. The curfew goals are written down and signed in contract form.

Let's look at each one of them closer. Curfews must be earned until Jr. moves out or goes to college. It is important to tie curfew to behavior because it puts the burden on him and off you. What you use as markers is up to your particular situation. You may want to target specific behaviors. To me, academic performance is a given and should be included in any contract. If you're puzzled about what to use as markers, just think of what disturbs you the most about your teen.

Following are examples of behavioral markers that can increase or decrease freedom. Negative outcomes are regular font and positive outcomes are emphasized:

If John receives all C's and above on his report card then he will be able to stay out until 10.00 on weekends and he will be able to hang out with his friends until 5:00 on school nights. For each grade below a C John receives he will lose two hours of curfew time on each night.

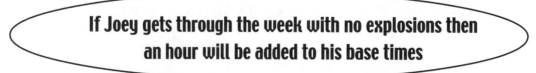

If John receives all grades above a C with a B+ average then he will have one hour added to his base time.

Joey's base time is 10:00 on weekend nights and 5:00 on weekday nights. For each rude verbal outburst Joey implements he will lose one hour off each night. For Example, if Joey explodes at his parents then his base time will be moved up to 9:00 on weekends and 4:00 on weekdays.

If Joey gets through the week with no explosions then an hour will be added to his base times

Laura will be at preapproved supervised locations when out on weekends. These may be multiple locations but there must be an adult on the premises (football games, movies, and friend's house.) If Laura lies about where she is going or where she has been she will not be allowed out at all the following week.

If Laura maintains her proposed schedule and explains her whereabouts in an honest manner then she will earn one half hour on all her base times.

It is important to put what I call "accountability extensions" on the curfew. This gives your child incentive to spend time in healthier places. Here you are pitting one urge against the other. You have placed your teens desire to be unsupervised in conflict with their desire for a later curfew. This is important. To earn the later curfew they must be at a supervised location and be able to prove they are there.

It is important to raise the level of accountability if the group is co-ed. Besides the obvious reasons there are some that are subtler. By changing expectations when your child is out in a co-ed setting you are saying, "This is different, this is important, I believe that this situation requires more foresight. Because of the possibility of sex occurring, I'm requiring you to be more accountable and spend more time in supervised situations while you are out." Just like other strategies, you may not be saying it verbally, but you are saying it with your actions.

The "Trust Thing"

If you haven't already heard it then you will hear it eventually. "Don't you trust me?" You are going to screen boyfriends, set curfews, check out music choices, and possibly, if you feel it's necessary, search rooms. Doesn't this show a lack of trust? No, it shows good parenting. When you limit movie choices and set curfews you are protecting your teen. When you parent permissively you are violating the trust your teen has in you.

Your teen needs to trust you. He needs to know that you care and that you will put up with his abuse to protect him. He doesn't know he trusts you to do this. It's just there. He trusted you to feed him when he could not feed himself. He trusted you to stop him from crossing the street in traffic. And now he trusts you to protect him from himself until he can protect himself from himself. He trusts you to protect him from sexual situations. When he shows over a period of time that he can trust himself to protect himself then you can trust him. And then you can show that trust by discontinuing the monitoring that he needed you to do.

Has your child earned your trust?

You will not have to play this game forever. Eventually you will have a teenager who will make the right choices because it's the right thing to do. But we're not there yet. It is important to let him know that if he meets the above expectations for a long period of time, you will relax your monitoring.

In other words, for you to "lay off" he must earn your trust over a long period of time. So if he tells you that he will be at the Smiths at 10:00 and he's not there when you called, he's lost trust as well as time from his curfew.

The more consistently he meets your expectations the less monitoring you will need to do. As you implement the strategies in this book you may feel like Robocop. But eventually you will be able to ease up because you have retrained your child. And more importantly, your child has gained your trust. Don't get too excited, this could take years.

You have probably figured out by now that much of what I'm going to ask you to do in this book will benefit your family in many ways. Setting time and place parameters on your child will not only reduce the risk of sexual activity, it will also reduce the risk of drug and alcohol involvement, street violence, property damage and all the other wonderful activities teens find themselves in when given too much time too soon.

In this chapter I have introduced a skill you must master. This skill is profound in its simplicity. It is an incredible template for teen control and will help you in guiding your teen through the sexual minefield that is adolescence. What is this technique that you will benefit from? What is one of the verbal keys to good teen management? What method will help guide your teen to a healthy adulthood? I call it the "if/then statement." Sounds incredibly easy doesn't it? Believe me, using if/then statements will help you.

If..........Then......

You can see the *if/then* statement at work in the curfew examples. The *if/then* statement works on an algebraic concept. Or perhaps you can think of it as physics principal. You know the one: every action has an equal and opposite reaction. Let's take a closer look at *"if...then"*

If you stay out with Jennifer past curfew tonight, *then* you will have to have her come over here and stay in this house when you want to see her.

If you visit another pornographic web site, *then* you will lose complete use of the computer.

If you insist on wearing clothing that stresses your bust line, *then* we will have to assume you are not using good judgement in other areas and you will have to be in earlier.

If we find any more pornographic material in your room or in your book bag, *then* you will be grounded for one month.

The *If-then* statements can also be stated in positive terms.

If you continue to handle yourself in a mature manner while out, *then* we will stop requiring you to give us a play by play itinerary before you go out.

If you continue making good social decisions *then* we will give you more access to the car.

You get the idea. The if/then statement is your friend. Use it. What will eventually happen is that your child will internalize the if/then statement. It will work something like this. He will be at a party, someone will offer him a drink and he will think, *"If* I get drunk *then* I may seriously hurt myself and people that I care about."* If/then will also help on the sexual front, *"If* I have sex tonight *then* I may get pregnant."* If /then trains young people to think in terms of action/ consequence. This will help them resist sexual temptation as well as help then in general decision making.

Teaching your teen If/then thinking will help on the sexual front.

When setting expectations with your teen communicate and summarize in if-then statements. Remember; If-then is your friend.

By communicating with if/then statements you are using the simple idea that a man will reap what he sows. Instead of "reaping" and "sowing" you're using "if" and "then." You will make clear connections between action and consequence. We will see later in this book how the media has blurred the line between reality and fantasy in regards to consequences. In your teen's sex saturated media world there are no consequences for teen sex. As a matter of fact there are no negative consequences for anything. Use If / then to get your teen to think in terms of action – consequence.

**Use if/then to get your teen thinking
in terms of action – consequence.**

To be a healthy adult your teen must learn to regard actions in relation to the consequences which result from those actions. Once again I'm tying teen sexual behavior to larger cultural behavior patterns. If a teen suffers no consequences for staying out past curfew, doing drugs, talking back to parents, and being disrespectful to teachers why should he expect to suffer consequences from having sex? Let me try to relate the larger behavior trends to sexual trends another way. If a teen is able to misbehave at school and at home and suffer no negative consequences, then doesn't it make sense that he will take his chances and misbehave sexually?

Or perhaps we should use different language. If we have allowed our children to live without limits why should we expect them to limit themselves sexually?

**If we allow our children to live
without time and behavior limits
why should we expect them to
limit themselves sexually?**

Set curfews. Set parameters. Narrow the window.
Allow your child to earn the freedom he thinks he deserves.
Use curfews to teach the law of reaping and sowing.

If you think you have an understanding of these chapters then get your "Bucky" and lay down the law. You will find the appropriate template and instructions in Appendix B (Fig R.7 and R.8). I suggest you write everything down in order to protect family tranquility.

If/then statements are your friend. If you have been using emotion and argument to control your teen you need to switch to a calm If/Then approach. Go to the reproducible chapter and cut out the poster on R.9. Place it by your mirror to remind you to stop shouting and use If/Then.

Action Plan

As a result of reading this chapter what are you going to do and when are you going to do it?

Examples - *I will get together with my spouse and discuss curfews.*

We will make out a curfew contract on ____/____/_____

_____

_____

_____

_____

_____

_____

_____

_____

_____

_____

_____

_____

_____

_____

_____

_____

Kids are the way they are because of what they are exposed to.
— Joe White

Hiding leads nowhere except to more hiding.
— Margaret A. Robinson

CHAPTER 7

Sticks and Stones Will Break Their Bones and What They See and Hear Will Hurt Them

Let's try a little exercise. I'm going to say a phrase and you will say the next words that come into your mind, then you will turn the page to see what the right answer is.

Are you ready? Here we go.

HICKORY DICKORY DOCK...

Now, what came into your mind? "The mouse ran up the clock" right? How long has it been since you heard this little nursery rhyme? How many years? How many decades? How many eras? Yet, this senseless ditty lay forever embedded in your psyche and ready to be called up in an instant.

You haven't rehearsed nursery rhymes every five years for the last thirty years, yet this sense-less ditty stayed with you. It was a part of you. What's the point? Quite simply this: what you see and hear becomes a part of you.

If your children are continually exposed to sexual imagery and sexual audio they will internal-ize what they see and hear whether they want to or not.

You can't shrug off your responsibility to guard what they see and hear. You can't say it doesn't matter. You just proved that what goes in stays in.

Yes you guessed it. This chapter is going to be about the music your kids listen to and the TV they watch. But it's not that simple. Our parents had to worry about TV, radio and the theater. We have to worry about TV, radio, and cable, video, the Internet; cell phones, CDs, and the cinema, in short, teen targeted media. There is no way that what they are seeing and hearing isn't affecting their sexual behavior or sexual worldview. No way.

The average American child (ages 2 to 11) watches approximately 28 hours per week of television. Teens watch television approximately 23 hours per week.[1]

The evidence that violent and sexual media content does affect behavior is overwhelming. It's just not getting much airtime. Why? Well think about it. Ten major companies own all the TV outlets. Do you think they are going to promote the idea that too much sexual and violent content begets negative behavior in teens? Can you see MTV running a special on how sexual imagery desensitizes youth to real world sexual behavior? Would HBO run a story on the con-nection between increased teen sexual experimentation and exposure to sexual material? Would they run it before or after *"Sex in the City?"*

Think about it. Is it a coincidence that the Columbine Killers spent all their time listening to Marilyn Manson and playing Doom? Do you think that it's a coincidence that all of the teen school killers of the past four years listened to death rock and were first person shooter addicts? What our kids are seeing and hearing is affecting them. Just pick up the newspaper.

By the time the average child graduates from high school, they will have seen between 240,000 to 480,000 sexual acts or references to sex.[2] Portrayal of premarital fornication on TV outnumbers marital sexual situations <u>eight to one</u>.[3]

Hypothetical . . .
If all you're seeing promotes casual premarital sex and all you're hearing promotes premarital sex, then wouldn't it be normal to engage in premarital sex?

Let's rephrase the question. Teens are exposed to sex saturated media 28 hours a week and spend less than three minutes a week in meaningful conversation with an adult. They hear "have sex" for twenty-eight hours and don't have sex (if they hear it at all) for a few minutes a week. In this situation which source is more likely to influence their decision when the choice has to be made?

What does all the above have to do with your teen's sexual behavior? Everything. Why am I going to continue to make the case that sexual media will influence their behavior? Because I know that some of you have bought the lie that what teens are exposed to is harmless.

I also know that this strategy is going to be one of the hardest for you to implement. So before we go into *how* to protect your child we must continue to go into *why* it's important.

I know you don't want to monitor what goes in your child's eyes and ears. I know you don't want to hold yourself responsible for what they see and hear. It will take so much energy and create conflict. Reread chapter three and press on.

See, I know you really don't want to do this. You don't want to tell your daughter that she can't go to that movie that contains "nudity and graphic imagery," but you have to.

You don't want to go through your son's CD collection but you need to. You don't want to limit TV viewing but it's crucial.

You don't want to monitor video rentals. But you must.

You don't want to be the "only parents" that won't let your daughter go to a concert, But...

Understand this. The idea that sex is sacred and should be limited to marriage is under attack. The approach that will keep your child healthy - abstinence until marriage and monogamy afterward - is being pummeled by teen targeted media. (T.T.M, pronounced tem)

"Where is this happening?" you think. "What assault?" you ask. The assault that is taking place within youth targeted media. You may not notice the anti family bias while watching TV, but you're watching *Sixty Minutes.* You may think you know the extent of sex saturation in *teen* targeted media, but you don't. Watch some of *their* programming. Listen to some of *their* music, go into some of *their* chat rooms, and read some of *their* magazines.

Every once and a while I slap on my fins, mask, and wet suit (so nothing sticks to me) to take a swim in teen culture. I have to do it to stay current with their world and to keep my comedy shows sharp and focused. I need to know what the enemy is doing so I can defend and attack. If I loose touch with my target audience I lose impact. So, once a quarter I force myself to watch *Total Request Live* on MTV, read their magazines and poke around in their sex-saturated world. Considering the world we give them, America's teens are holding up quite well... considering the world we give them.

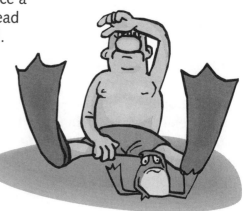

The band Slipknot is also indicative of what is out there. Not only is teen sex promoted, so is sadomasochism. Their lyrics contain such uplifting tidbits as ("I want to cut your throat and f— the slit.") On the title track of their new album, Iowa, the singer murders his girlfriend in a sick act of fondness ("I will kill you to love you"). This gem contains another track called "People = S—" ("I got changed and I'm sitting on the side of Satan"). You're thinking such lyrics must appeal to just a fringe element of our youth. Just the freaks, right? Not the kids that live in your neighborhood. Right? Wrong.

Slipknot's 1999 self-titled Roadrunner debut has sold three million copies and hit number one on Billboard's charts. After my shows and during retreats I conduct, youth often question me about Slipknot and other hate bands. These kids often ask, "Is it 'Ok' to listen to Slipknot?" Or the classic question posed as a statement, "It's just music, I don't really believe in it." The fact that they own the CD (most likely bought with money given to them by their parents) is disturbing. The fact that they need to ask the question is more so.

Slipknot is a heavy metal hate band. They should be expected to be disgusting, right? Other types of teen music aren't as sexually graphic, Right? Wrong. These "have sex, Satan rules, do what you want, and wrong is right" messages run through all types of teen targeted music. On his rhythm and blues album an artist called Afroman plies his art over a great rhythm section. Too bad he sings about the benefits of drugs and perverted sex. A cut off his CD called, "The Good Times" tells the story of a series of encounters involving anal sex, oral sex, and sleeping with a cross-dressing man.

What about TV? The Fox series, "Undeclared" is typical of teen targeted TV. Undeclared follows the adventures of a boy's first year at college. In the first episode our hero, Steven, has sex with a girl from his dorm. They have sex after the following deep conversation:

"You know what we should do? We should have sex!"

"Oh yeah."

"Yeah, for fun. Do you have a condom?"

"I have *eight* condoms!"

This theme runs through youth media. You're an animal, and it's natural for you to have sex. Sometimes it's flatly stated and sometimes it's suggested. But the message is always the same. Sex is natural, sex for you now is natural, and sex equals love.

The idea that teen targeted media affects their behavior is well supported and documented. It's just not getting much airtime. The Kaiser Family Foundation reported that the **"media's love affair with sex and romance contributes to irresponsible sexual behavior among young people, including unplanned and unwanted pregnancies"**[5]

There is a very deep and profound statement given to us anonymously from a guru that lived among the ancients. The observation is "Garbage in, Garbage out."

Joe White sums up what I'm hoping to get across in his book, *What Kids Wish Parents Knew About Parenting*: It all adds up to one overreaching observation: Children become what they think about. And they think about what they see and hear. Kids are the way they are because of what they are exposed to, what they fill their minds with.[6]

Strategies to Fight Back

We'll start with TV, because TV viewing is the easiest to monitor. Now, you need to look at this battle as one you can at worst influence and at best win. There are two fronts that you will fight on. You will control devices and the content that comes through the devices. You see, you have a great advantage in this battle. Most teen targeted media needs a device to get to your teen.

1. You will control the placement and access to devices.

2. You will control the content that comes through those devices.

Movies need theaters, disc players and TVs. Chat rooms and internet pornography need computers, internet connections and monitors. Music needs TV, radio, CD players, computers and the internet. Sexual imagery needs a magazine, book or screen to be presented on.

Isn't this great! All the teen targeted "have sex" messages need a physical device to get into your home and into your kid's mind.

Control the devices and you control the message!

You see, the battle is winnable. Parents constantly approach me and ask the wrong question: "What can I do about all the pornography/sexual music/sexual programming that's out there?" No wonder they feel overwhelmed. You can't take on teen targeted media. You can't stop Madison Avenue from writing sexually manipulating material; you can stop that material from entering your home. You can't control the creation of content; you can control your child's access to that content.

Let me define the way I'm using these two words:

Content - *The ideas and images* that are viewed or listened to (or both). Ex. The Thong Song, Eyes Wide Shut, pornographic imagery, safe sex propaganda, pro abortion essays, birth control advertisements, music that graphically encourages teens to be sexually active, shows that feature teen sex as a major theme. etc.

Devices - *The physical contraption* (which you may or may not know how to use) that those ideas and images (content) travel through to your teen. Ex. TVs, cinemas, CD players, computers, books, magazines, radios, car stereos, and any physical contraption that hasn't been invented at the printing of this book. In other words, I'm putting into this category all the things that content travels through or on.

Now, work with me here. If you get this point you will be more inspired to fight this battle. Any time you can divide an enemy it is to your advantage. The TV is a device; the Playboy Channel can provide content to come through the TV. The movie, *Eyes Wide Shut* is content. The content needs a device, a theater, video player or DVD player, to get to your child. Howard Stern creates anti family content that needs a radio or a TV to get to your kid. Eminem creates content that needs a device - radio or CD player to get to your kid. Pornographers create sites (content) that need a computer, to get to your kid.

Parents approach me and ask, "What do I do about all the stuff that's out there?" You can do very little, if anything, about all the stuff that's *out there*.

You can not stop the creation of sexually explicit material, anti family messages, pro casual sex imagery, teen targeted sexual manipulation, pornography, pro casual sex music, videos, articles and imagery. In short, you can't stop the creation of content.

Some of you believe to make a difference you must take on all the content creators. No wonder you feel helpless. In his cutting edge book, *Right From Wrong*, Josh McDowell nicely sums up what I'm trying to get at: "We must not expect to change our culture (if indeed we could); we must change the way we respond to it. It does no good to bemoan our society; we must control how much we allow it to influence our children."[7]

> **You may not be able to control the content but you CAN control your child's exposure to that content.**

The TV

Let me give you a simple example of "device control."

Control the placement and access to the TV in your house. Now I'm not talking about what comes through it yet, just the stupid black box itself. Where is it and how do people get to it?

Once again, I must regress. Some of you, upon reading the previous sentence, thought, *placement of TV? Doesn't he mean placement of TVs?*

Unfortunately, most American homes have more than one TV. In fact, many American young people have TVs in their own bedrooms.

> **If your child has a TV in his bedroom, you're wrong.**
> **If your child has a TV in his bedroom with a cable or satellite connection, you're more wrong.**
> **If your child has a TV in his room with cable and a video/DVD player, you're very, very wrong.**
> **That's it, period.**

I've heard all kinds of excuses and rationalizations so give it up. The one I hear most often is, "I monitor his viewing." Yeah right. You may monitor his viewing some of the time. But, lets face it, you're old. You need sleep.

Your kids have you "timed." (The same way prisoners know when the guards make their rounds) They know when you go to sleep. And what's even scarier, they know when you go into deep sleep. They learn this early on. *Lets see, if I sneak into the kitchen to get an Elmo cookie right after Mommy goes into her bedroom, Mommy hears me. But if I wait a little longer Mommy does not hear me.*

That TV is on long after you've checked in. And you have no idea what they're watching. No idea. Even if there is no cable hookup he can get into plenty of trouble. Don't take my word for it. Stay up past your bedtime and check out the network stations.

If there is a video player hooked up to your teen's TV then his viewing options are limitless. Oh, I know what you just thought. You thought, "We don't have any sexually explicit videos in our home." *You* don't have to have any damaging material for his video/DVD player to be dangerous. Kids trade videos at school. When I was a sixth grade teacher I cracked many "video-trading rings." Usually one kid gains access to an R or X-rated video. He may have discovered his dad's stash or a store or flea market that will let him buy. It doesn't matter. He gets his hands on the stuff. He then plays the hero in school by distributing it to classmates. They may go home right after school and view before you get home.

I confiscated quite a few videos when I taught. When the parents were called I always got the same response, "I have no idea where he got that." Often, I got the feeling that Mom was telling the truth. Dad, on the other hand.... I've actually had parents angry with me for finding this stuff on their child or in their child's locker. "What were you doing searching his locker?" I then explain that it's the school's locker and the student gets to use it ten months out of the year.

I've been out of the classroom since the advent of DVD. These discs must present quite a problem. They are much smaller than videos and much easier to conceal. If you don't have the gumption to take the TV out of your childs bedroom, at least take the video/DVD player out and disconnect the cable.

If there is cable or satellite in his bedroom, I have to ask, "What were you thinking?" I'm sorry; I didn't mean to lose it there. In spite of all the children and parents I've worked with, I still get emotional about parent's behavior. I've had kids swear at me, try to hurt me, threaten my life, get pregnant, get someone pregnant, get a disease, give a disease, lie to me, allow themselves to be transported by me while carrying drugs, and basically abuse me. I've never gotten angry or expressed anger towards them. Frustrated yes, furious no.

Parents, on the other hand, can infuriate me. It amazes me when I turn on the TV and hear experts pontificate on our "sick" children. We're the ones who are crazy. If the children are sick then the parents are simply demented.

Americans can't eat a meal without TV

Parents surrender their children to all kinds of violent and sexual imagery and then expect them to be "normal." That's insane. They farm them out, submit them to serial marriages or unstable living arrangements, force feed them garbage and expect to reap a healthy child. That's crazy.

Let's take a break and I will give you a snapshot of some of the parental insanity I've dealt with during my in home-counseling and teaching career. Perhaps you will recognize yourself:

I once stood on the back deck of a home discussing the erratic and violent behavior of an eleven-year-old boy. One of the things the parent wanted me to address was the child's new smoking habit. The parent was smoking during this conversation. She declared between puffs, "I'm very concerned that he has started smoking." We were on the deck because the parent was "very responsible and never smoked in the home." Insane.

I once spent several sessions working with a father on the issues of his daughter's sexual promiscuity and occult interests. His live in girlfriend always sat in on these sessions because she was very concerned. (This was live in girlfriend number two; live in girlfriend number one never showed much interest.) Insane.

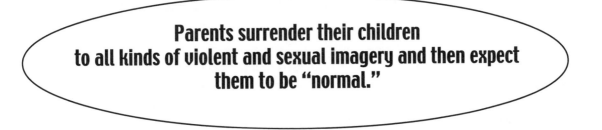

Parents surrender their children to all kinds of violent and sexual imagery and then expect them to be "normal."

I once had a conversation with a married couple (occasionally I run into them) who was concerned about their third grader's low impulse control and violent physical/verbal outbursts. While we were having this conversation in the kitchen I could see the third-grader in the den playing *Mortal Combat II*. He was doing very well. His character had just delivered a "death blow" or "finishing move." When the player the boy is controlling completes this move he gets to rip off the head of his foe while blood spurts out of the stump. Part of the spine is also pulled out of the body with the head. Nice touch. Insane.

I worked with a family that had six TVs in their home. Six. They had hired me because their teen's grades had dropped and they had discovered a joint and condoms in his jacket. He turned out to have a TV with cable in his room. What a surprise. During one of our sessions I asked, "What programming does he have access to?"

"Just the standard package."
"What's in the standard package," I asked.
"Well you know, just what you get when you add another TV and buy cable."
"I don't know, I don't have cable," I replied.
"Well...it's got one hundred and four channels.. So...

It became apparent that the parents didn't know. We went upstairs and went through his "choices." Soon we were watching cheerleaders that did not seem to be connected to any sanctioned sport I'm familiar with. The parents were somewhat chagrinned. They didn't know. Think about it, they didn't know. Insane.

Are you insane? Well are you? It is insane to allow devices to transport violent and pornographic imagery into your home. It is even crazier to allow it into your child's bedroom. Now here is the ultimate insanity, what absolutely sets me off: when parents expose their kids to this *garbage* and expect *positive* results. That's really insane.

> # The adults of America are truly ill. The high drug use and promiscuous sexual behavior of our children are simply symptoms of a national epidemic of parental insanity.

Please excuse my bit of venting. Let's get back to "black box control." I was talking about the importance of controlling TV viewing when I went off on my "parental Insanity" tirade. Are you ready for this big step? Are you ready to take on the giant industries that shovel violence and porn into your teen's mind? Remove the TV from his room. Wow, you have defeated the purveyors of porn. You didn't form a lobby group, write a congressman, go on a talk show, protest on the capitol steps, or march. You did something more effective. You removed the device.

One of the excuses I hear from parents is, "We never want to watch the same program." Of course you don't. If you did I'd be worried. Whatever happened to arguing and negotiating? What is so unhealthy about disagreeing? What about give and take? No wonder the generation we are bringing up is unable to deal with discord or disagreement; they have never been exposed to it. Many kids don't know how to negotiate because they never had to negotiate at home. Some haven't even been forced to sit through *Sixty Minutes* or a presidential speech with their parents.

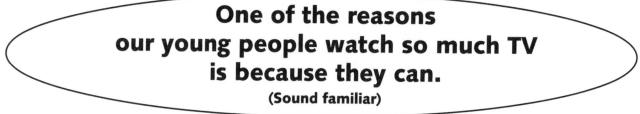

> # One of the reasons our young people watch so much TV is because they can.
> ### (Sound familiar)

They get to watch what they want when they want to. One of the reasons is because they have access to multiple TVs. This is an easy one to solve folks. Get rid of some of your TVs and move the remaining one to a "public" room. The one in your childs room has to go, but the one in the basement might also be up for grabs, especially if it has cable.

The idea here is that TV viewing takes place in a location that can be periodically and easily monitored. You're looking for a location that you pass through frequently. Now this is important. You haven't set times, tried to control programming or implemented any other high effort strategy. You have simply reduced the number of TV's in the house and controlled the location of the remaining one. By simply doing this you have cut teen TV viewing in half.

Your kid is going to hate you for taking "his" TV. (Let's face it, you bought it. But even if he bought it, it's got to come out. You can buy it back.) If your child really freaks out when you remove *your* TV from his room do you think he had a little dependency thing going on? In other words, the stronger the protest, the stronger the addiction.

When addicts are confronted with their drug use they deny. *Mom, you don't have to take it out, I don't watch it that much.* When cut off from the drug they protest violently. The depth of the addiction can be judged by the intensity of the protest.

All you're doing is taking the TV from his room. You're not separating him from food or denying him air. If he responds as if you are, then he has an unhealthy addiction. Did you have a TV in your bedroom when you were growing up? Neither did I. Why have we allowed our children to believe they have a right to a TV in their room? You didn't have one and you didn't come out particularly scarred. Take it out. That's it, period. Remember that he's still going to have access to the "common area TV." Now if none of your children have their own TV, bear with me. We'll get to you.

As much as you can, make taking out the TV a positive event. It is a positive event. Now here are some things you can do:

1. Donate the TV and VCR to a local nonprofit. Make a big deal about it so that your child will be proud.

2. Sell the TV and give the money to Jr.

3. Sell the TV and use the money for one of the following activities.
   A. Throw a party for a group (who knows, you may start a movement)

   B. Go on a family trip to a destination picked by the TV donator

   C. Send the TV donator on a trip or to a camp.

   D. Match the income from the TV sale. We could call this a matching grant. Now with this larger amount of money you could do something really cool. You could buy a mountain bike or some other big-ticket item.

If you are getting off cable (kind of like getting off heroin) you will be saving on a monthly fee. The money you will be saving on a monthly basis presents a wonderful incentive opportunity. Tell your teen you will use "matching funds" to go on a monthly adventure.

You can make this monthly adventure even more appealing by taking it during a school day. Obviously, you would do this only if his grades are acceptable. If you don't want him to have an absence on his schedule, pick him up after 12:00. Most school districts will count him for a full day if he stays to noon.

This can be very effective. Whenever he/she whines about his TVless room, or not having cable in the house, you can point out that one of your adventures is coming up. Remember that you don't have to do any of this. You're the parent. You can simply take the surplus TVs out of the house and move the sole survivor to the living room. But if your child is an addict, he will go through something very similar to heroin withdrawal. Any creative way you can make this easier for him is worth the effort.

So, now that the TV is out of his room, you are done dealing with the TV issue. **Wrong.** You still have to deal with any other TV in a covert location. The kid's TV should be in a room that can be monitored.

That's right; siblings will actually monitor each other. Think of it. What boy wants to be caught by his sister watching porn or any other program that parents have ruled out? By simply eliminating TV's that are in remote locations you have dealt a serious blow to the forces that battle for your child's mind. There will be several other positive side effects to getting the TV out of his room. You will see him more often. (Remember this is a good thing). He will have to develop alternatives to TV for entertainment (perhaps these alternatives will require actual communication or the use of his mind). He will lose the ash white complexion and stoned TV stare. His attention span will lengthen. And his chance for exposure to sexually explicit material will decrease.

It would be ideal if you could get down to one TV in a common area. What do we mean by a common area? Just that. The kid's TV or family TV should be in a place that people pass through on a regular basis. It should be "common" to every member of the household.

Now that you have limited the number of TVs you must control the ones that remain. You have several options. You're concerned about TV viewing when you aren't home or when you're asleep. You aren't finished. You must control the TVs that survived the purge. Remember, when you control this one particular "device" you are also controlling the cable, video, and gaming gadgets that need the TV to deliver content.

Let's look at a few more strategies that still fall under "device control." You can use an **electronic plug box.** This is just what the name implies. It's a fantastically insidious little contraption that locks up the plug to your TV (or any other electronic device). It's about as low tech as you can get. It's simple and fast. It's a neat clean little box that goes around the plug and locks. There, you don't have to worry about *that* TV. This device can come into play while you're at work or at home. If you just can't get rid of the TV in the basement then "lock it." You can get more information on the plug box at electronicplugbox.com. The cost is 18.99. The advantages of this strategy are the low cost and the simplicity. There is obviously no monthly fee once you buy the box. Though it is simple to operate, it is manual. It will need you and your key to work. Your children will have to ask you to unlock the TV when they want to view it, and you will have to remember to lock it back up.

You can also lock them out of the TV using a strategy supplied by your cable provider. Call your cable provider and see what is available. Because there are so many different cable companies and contracts out there, I can't give out specific information for each one. At the writing of this book, almost every cable company offers ways to lock your child out of "the box." Some provide a physical key: others provide a computer code to disable the cable (and hence the TV), for a certain period of time each day.

Call your cable or satellite company and bug them about this. Most companies do not promote disabling features in their literature. The stations they carry don't want them to. I hate to sound like a conspiracy theorist but if you think about it, it makes sense. Bug them and they will tell you how to control cable access when you are not home. Threaten to switch services and they will mail you instructions or give out a web address that has detailed disabling steps.

Threaten to switch cable/satellite providers and they will mail you instructions or give out a web address that has detailed disabling steps.

Now we are going to move to content control. Thus far we have only considered device control. In this case we have discussed controlling the location of the TV and when it comes on or off, or whether it comes on at all. Pretty simple huh? Compared to Device control content control usually takes more time and money to implement. Your options for filtering what's coming through your TV are limited.

We are now moving to what comes through your TV once it's on. One simple way of controlling content is limiting options. With the TV, it's simply a matter of limiting viewing options to the traditional networks. What a Whiz-Bang High Technology strategy for protecting your children from sexual desensitization: disconnect cable! That's right, no cable or satellite. Just ABC, CBS, NBC, Fox, and PBS. They won't be able to watch the R or X rated options if they bypass your other strategies because the options won't be there. At worst, they will be limited to Baywatch reruns.

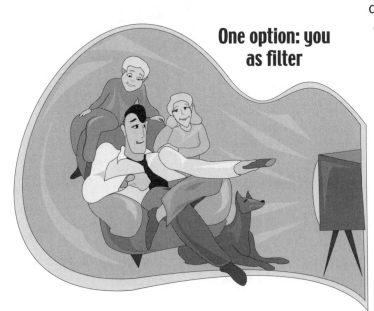

One option: you as filter

I'm assuming you are already on cable or satellite. Most of the families I work with are. Most of America is. I have never had cable, satellite or anything else my whole adult life. I've been told it is extremely difficult to "get off" or "give up" cable service. I can honestly say I can't speak to that difficulty because Julia and I have never had to kick the habit. We've never been on.

Not only do they have ways to control whether your cable is on or off. (And hence your TV), they can control what comes through when it is on. So the cable (and satellite companies) may be able to help with both device (access or not at certain times), and content control (filtering what comes through).

Cable and Satellite companies can help you control both access and content.

When you signed up for cable you picked a package. That package probably contains some viewing options you don't want Jr. to have. Movie channels can be the worst. What they run at midday may be acceptable, but what they run at night or early in the morning is usually not.

Some movie channels specialize in what they term "adult programming." You don't have to get the whole package. You may ask the company to block certain stations and options from coming through. Bug them and they will do this for you. Trust me, they can do this. Now what's the catch? It will usually cost you more money to get fewer channels! However do try to negotiate by threatening to switch providers or technologies. ("At that fee I'll be forced to go to cable." or "At that fee I'll be forced to switch to satellite.")

My mommy took my cable

You have two options with your current cable/satellite service. Clean it up or get rid of it. The provider can help you clean it up, but it may cost you. Your children are worth it, aren't they? If you don't want to pull the plug on your precious history channel or multiple sports channels, call the company. They should be able to help. If they can't or won't, cancel. You can do it! Use the monthly fee you're saving to *go* to a few *actual* historical sites or sports events.

Before you go into cable/satellite pre-withdrawal, I have more content control options. If you can't get your cable/satellite provider to clean up its act, consider switching to a pre-sanitized provider. **Sky Angel Satellite** is a good example of clean alternatives that are out there. You will still have satellite; it just won't be the provider "everybody else has." **Sky Angel** provides family cartoons, puppets, game shows, talk shows and music video programs.

Sky Angel also carries family radio stations targeted to teens. This is a valuable service if you live in a part of the nation that is not served by family radio. **Sky Angel** can work with your current cable or satellite or you can drop your current provider and go with **Sky Angel** or a similar service alone. More information on **Sky Angel** can be found at www.skyangel.com.

By the time this book hits the stands, more alternatives for TV control will have emerged. Now that you know they are out there, get looking. Remember, strategies for controlling Teen Targeted Media range from the simple to the complex, you may not have decided how to deal with cable yet. But darn it, at least limit viewing time and get that TV out of his/her room. Start simple. What are you waiting for? Are you home alone and don't have the strength to start moving TVs by yourself? Sneak down the hall and unplug the cable and make off with the VCR. After the screams die down you will sleep better.

> **Now that you know there are options for TV control out there, get looking.
> One will be right for you and your family.**

**Who me?
I don't stare**

Sexual ideas start in the eyes and move to the mind. It starts by looking. We must be visually tempted before we act on what our brains create. When I say "we," I mean unfortunately, men. Men are wired visually. If this sounds like an anti-male statement, its not. It's just the way we are made. Women feel what men see. Think about it. You don't see women line up to watch men dance naked or buying magazines featuring naked men.

Can looking lead to lust? Yes. Can continuous looking lead to lust? Yes. Can a fourteen-year-old boy, who watches pornography on TV, raids his father's magazine stash, and has unlimited access to sexual imagery develop an unhealthy attitude towards females? Absolutely, positively, yes. Such a boy will view girls as physical objects because that's how he's been exposed to them.

A special note to fathers

Fathers, you need to model respect for women. If you have the *Sports Illustrated* Swimsuit calendar over your workbench, take it down. If you have any advertisements featuring anatomically disproportionate women hanging around your house get rid of them. Not only should you protect your children's eyes but you also should protect your own.

I've never been inside Hooters. Let's face it, they don't sell chicken there. Do I think I will run naked and throw rocks if I step inside Hooters and order wings from a top-heavy waitress wearing orange shorts two sizes to small? No. Will I suddenly feel the need to have an affair? No. But why submit my eyes to the visual temptation? Why give my wife the visual competition? Men, lets face it. Your eyes are your primary sexual organs. Do you protect them and discipline them? Are you modeling positive behavior for your son and daughter or are you teaching your son to look upon women as physical objects and your daugher to become one?

Men, you may have to clean your own house before you go into your teenager's room. Dad, your children watch and listen to you more than you know. You thought you only had to worry about your wife catching you staring (or should I say leering), but now you have to worry about your son. Or don't worry about anybody and stop staring/leering.

Purity Covenant

Men, can you spend one hour with your son? Can you spend two hours one on one? Do you want to take two hours from your life and make a powerful gesture that your son will remember forever? Go to the reproducible section (located in the back of this book) and make two copies of the Purity Covenant form. (R.10) Call up one of your buddies who also has a son about the same age and arrange to go out to eat.

Share with your friend what is in your heart and what you would like to do. It would be ideal if he has also read the book but it is not necessary. The principles this exercise is based on are easy to understand and the need for it is clear. Meet and have a great time together. Towards the end of the meal break out the two forms and "teach on them." After discussion, sign the forms. Each father-son team will then have a form with four signatures on it. Remember, you are not teaching a complex lesson. Discussion and signing of the form should take fifteen minutes at the most. But, though your overall time together should be casual those fifteen minutes should be serious.

Now men, with two hours of your time (counting from the time you left the driveway until the time you got home) you have made a powerful statement in too many ways to list. You also have an instant father/son accountability group. No, you don't have to run this as intensely as other men's accountability groups. But you should still account. Once a month get together with the other father-son team and hang out. The majority of the time you spend together should be recreational. But the boys know why you have gotten together. Some time during the day, maybe while waiting in line for the go-karts or the batting cage, you look at your son and ask, "So how did you do with your eyes this month, buddy? Did you have a tough time on the beach trip?" And take it from there.

Action Plan

As a result of reading this chapter what are you going to do and when are you going to do it?

Examples - I will sit down with Josh, talk about "eye discipline" and fill out the Covenant Form (R-10) this Weds _____/_____/_____

We will talk with Joey and disconnect the cable from his room on _____/_____/_____. We will negotiate a vacation plan and take the TV out _____/_____/_____

_____

_____

_____

_____

_____

_____

_____

_____

_____

_____

_____

_____

_____

**If we don't stand up for children,
then we don't stand for much.**
– Marian Wright Edelman

**All that is necessary for evil to succeed is
that good men do nothing.**
– Edmund Burke

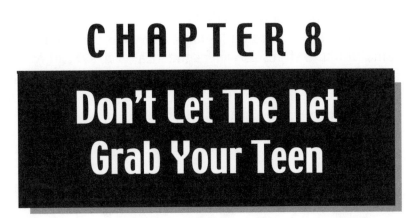

CHAPTER 8

Don't Let The Net Grab Your Teen

The World Wide Web is an incredible force for good. It allows doctors to diagnose across continents and a farmer in Dakota to discuss crop yields with a farmer in Germany.

The World Wide Web is also an incredible force for evil. Child prostitutes can be ordered online and contact information for the sex slave trade obtained. Your child can receive images of child rape, sadomasochism, bestiality, and "simple" pornography.

> **Whether the Internet is a force for evil or good in your home is up to you. You don't have to control the web. Just control your child's access to it and what he can get to when he gains that access.**

Once again, do not be intimidated by the web. You don't have to control the web. You just have to control your child's access to it. Just control the location of the device (in this case the computer) and the information that is allowed to come through the box. Control the device and control the content it carries.

Control the device and control the content it carries.

You have an idea of the simplicity of device control from the previous chapter. Apply the same common sense to monitor the computer as you did to the TV. A computer with net access should be in a physical space that can be monitored. You may have to give up convenience and aesthetics for safety. Yes, the computer does not look very good in your living room and you're sure Martha Stewart would disapprove, but that may be the exact place it needs to be. What about the foyer or kitchen or hall? Not all computers have to be so prominent in your interior design, just those with net access. Admittedly, there is nothing like the wires and off-white plastic of a computer to kill the ambiance of a room. But there are many solutions for the aesthetically minded. Buy a computer armoire. This concept takes the computer desk one step further. Think of it as a portable closet for your computer. When the computer is not in use, close the doors and the monitor, base, printer, and wires, are concealed from view.

Before you shudder at the thought of an additional "abstinence induced" cost, take heart. Computer closets/armoires range in price and quality as well as styles and finishes. They are available at brand name furniture stores as well as the local Wal/K/Stuff Mart. Of course, the ones from the Stuff Mart come in a box and have to be assembled. But hey, nobody has to know. And besides, this is the way Julia and I live. Our children are going to grow up believing that all furniture comes in a box with screws, bolts and instructions.

www.itmaynotbegoodforyourkids.com

Now that you have moved your computer, you are going to control its access to the net as well as what comes through it once that access is gained. You are probably beginning to realize that controlling the device itself (device control) is the easier part of the overall strategy to combat teen targeted media. It's easy to take or move one of the devices (radio, TV, stereo, CD, magazines, video). It takes more effort to control content once these devises are on.

You are going to control access to the net and what comes through it once access is gained. You are going to filter the content that comes through the net. Why do you want to do this? The question should really be why wouldn't you want to do this?

Are you already fearful? Do you feel the computer is beyond you? **If you have trouble setting an alarm clock you can still do what's necessary to make your computer safe.** I'm going to walk you through it step by step.

Before we tackle what to do we must continue to look at why we want to do it. If you think I'm trying to shock you into action, you're right.

Pornography is the most profitable web industry. While all the dot coms have struggled, net pornographers have marched on. And why wouldn't they? All they are selling is electronic imagery. They don't have to ship a product. They just have to post the imagery and charge people to look at it.

You may be thinking that your child would never seek out such material. Your child doesn't have to seek out pornography. Pornography will seek out your child. The mistake you may be making can be disastrous. Do not view the web as inert, static and inorganic. It is alive and always changing. Do not think of the web as online information or an electronic book. Think of it as a book that can manipulate, move and shove pages in front of you that you don't want to see and you definitely don't want your children to see.

My husband took down the swimsuit poster!

When I conduct my workshops, I often get the feeling parents just aren't getting it. They think internet porn consists of sending pictures of naked people back and forth on line. It's not something parents would condone but does Internet porn really require the alarmist response I advocate? In a word, yes. Research has shown that your child can stumble on "photographs and video clips depicting child rape, bestiality, sadomasochism, sexual abuse of the elderly and every other conceivable perversion."[1]

Would you open the door and allow a convicted pedophile into your home for some unsupervised playtime with your thirteen-year-old? Would you hand your child a magazine with images of bestiality and child rape? If you have an unfiltered net connection in your home then that's exactly what you're doing.

Pedophiles can "stalk" teen chat rooms. How do they do this? How do they stalk through a computer? Just the same way they stalk a potential victim at a park or school playground. Pedophiles are patient. They watch and build relationships over time. Pedophiles can enter teen oriented chat rooms anonymously and engage teens in real time "conversations." They build a relationship and then ask for a face to face meeting. This is why you insist that your child never meet a web contact face to face without a parent present. Emphasize this when you have your child sign the computer commandments. (R.11)

The net is a pedophile's playground. He can lurk in chat rooms posing as a child and arrange a meeting. He can transmit images to other pedophiles. He can even practice virtual molestation. There have been several documented cases of group molestation occurring on the net. Pedophiles actually use video conferencing to "share" their experiences. Using current net technology adults can even watch a rape from a remote location.

If you think I'm trying to prod you into action, you're right.

Pedophiles can get information from your teen. They have proven to be patient and familiar with teen language. They gain the information they need over weeks, months and in some cases years. During "fun" and "hip" conversations with your child they can learn real names, web and e-mail addresses, phone numbers, home address, and addresses for friends (thus increasing their potential prey database). They can even get school and family schedules. Yes, that's right. During innocent conversation within a teen chat room your child might be asked, "What time do your folks get in? Mine don't come home until 6:00 PM, that gives me time to chill and crank the music, how about yours?" Innocent enough if your child is talking to someone you know. Extremely dangerous if the "kid" asking the questions is a thirty five year old man who has gained your home address during previous "chats."

Before you rip your modem from the wall, let me jump ahead and assure you that you can fight online predators with the same tools you use to fight online porn. When you do get to the point, later in this chapter, where you chose or upgrade filterware, just remember to limit information from going out as well as coming in. Make sure you choose a strategy that allows you to limit chat room access. Also, be sure to block your children from giving out real time information about themselves.

I can do this, I can control net access

Children and teenagers love the Internet, and they should. They love to look things up, investigate, communicate, and discover. They learn how to use search engines almost immediately. And almost immediately, even if they are not looking for it, they will run into porn. Children are actually more likely than adults to experience "accidental viewing" because of the world they live in.

Adults are likely to punch in very specific words for the search engines, like "adjustable interest rates." Children and teenagers, on the other hand tend to type in words that bring on a broader or more open search. Let's say your seventh grader has to do a two-page report on dogs. He innocently enough types in "dogs". One in thirty of the responses or hits will be pornographic. Ex "young women with dogs and farm animals." How about a report on beavers? One in 25 will be pornographic and several of those will be hard core.[2]

Book reports also lead to trouble. If a child types in the title any one of children's favorites many and in some cases a majority of the responses will be sexual in nature. What about the classic children's book, "The Secret Garden." The word "secret" in the title will bring up web sites that contain sexual content. Louisa May Alcott's, "Little Women," another classic, would result in thousands of hits, among them the option of checking out, "hot little women." Because so many of teen's searches contain words like doll, toy, play, girl, boy, men, woman, and teenager, they are often confronted with pornography. They don't have to look for it. It looks for them.

This isn't what I was looking for, but ...

Once a teen is on a pornographic site he can choose to get off. Right. You would hope that your teen would get off. And he might. But why put him through the experience? "My teen can handle it" is the same kind of disastrous denial I mentioned in the beginning of the book. Remember, just because your teen is honest doesn't mean he is safe from sex. And just because your teen "is a good kid" does not mean he will choose to close pornographic sites when accidentally presented with one.

You need to filter out these sites. You need a filter. You need to install a filter, if you don't already have one. If you do have one, you need to update or upgrade it. If it is not upgradable you need a new one. Trust me. I'm being redundant, but I can't help it. This fix is easy.

Protect your on line child with a filtering strategy (filterware)

I will show you how to both install and upgrade. Actually, I will be a part of a team that will show you how to protect your computer. I'm too much of a computerphobe to explain the whole process as well as all your options. But before I do, I must warn you. Your kids are smarter than you are. At least with the computer. If you have an "old" filter they can figure out how to get around it or disarm it. If you have a "cheaper filter" they may have already messed it up.

I'm a technological idiot. It blows my mind to think that thirteen-year-olds can figure out how to "get around" an "old" filter. But they can. I'm going to suggest some filtering devices that are (at this writing) teen proof. But you are going to have to spend some time updating your filter or installing one. If the thought of installing anything on your computer makes you cringe, then read on. Don't be afraid.

Filters . . .

You are building and have been building a filtering device . . . the one located in your child's mind. Whether you know it or not, your child already has an internal filter. Ultimately, your goal is a child whose internal filter will keep him away from external garbage.

Everything you do in this book has the long-term goal of producing a young person who does not need you or your rules, or your games, or your contracts and curfews to do the right thing. But before he can internalize your value system, you must impose that value system. Then you can set him free.

Before he internalizes your value system you must impose that value system. Then set him free.

Eventually you will have a teenager who will filter out web garbage on his own. Until you get that teenager, you need to install a filtering program. If you have already done that you are going to check to see if your filterware is up to snuff. You are going to install an external filter (on his computer), so that his internal filter (his character) won't be tempted until it's developed.

Install a filter on the computer so that your child's internal filter (decision making/character) can grow.

Remember, you're not going to have to do this stuff forever. When they go off to college or leave home after high school you're done. It will be up to the internal filter that you built to take over. (Actually you should be done by mid senior year but if you haven't been doing this stuff you may be behind)

Now let's look at filterware. It doesn't matter whether you understand how the net works or not. It doesn't matter whether you think a server is found on a tennis court, a hard drive in your car or that memory is the thing that you are losing.

The job of a filtering device is to keep garbage out. This can get complicated so I'm going to simplify this for you. I will give you enough information for you to make a decision about your filtering options. But if you can't make a decision, I'm going to make one for you. I will decide to send you to a web site that will help you decide (or even decide for you). As you know, confusion leads to inaction, and if you're confused you will procrastinate updating your filtering device or installing one. I don't want you to do that. Procrastination in dealing with the net can be catastrophic for your family.

My decision will be to send you to web sites that will help you make a decision about filterware.

There are over 100 companies which offer products or services that monitor Internet content and regulate how the Internet is used in the home. Filters operate in two different ways. Some filter at the Server (The thing all the stuff goes through before it comes down the phone line to your computer). In other words they pre-filter the content before it gets to your computer. Other companies provide filters that are installed or downloaded right on the home computer and filter content after it enters.

So, you can sign up for a filter through your server. This is often referred to as server based filtering. Or you can buy filtering software and install it on your computer. This is often referred to as PC based blocking software. Or you could do nothing.

Don't do nothing. Do Something!

If you have an older computer (remember, "older" in computer language means anything-more than two years ago), it may have come with some type of filtering software. What it came with is not good enough. If you installed filtering software when you purchased it it's not good enough. Though it's infinitely better than doing nothing. You need a server-based program.

If you have no filtering tools, you need a server-based program.

If you have PC-based filtering software, you need a server-based program.

Why the preference? I'll explain. The first filtering devices to become available were installed on the user's computer to filter incoming online content. That means you bought software and downloaded it onto your computer (PC based filter ware). These programs did a good job. They were better than nothing was and they are better than nothing is.

Then came the next generation . . . server-based filters. They are installed on the server. No, you don't have to drive to some building filled with large computers. You sign up for it online, through your service provider. What are the advantages of server based filters over PC based software?

The first is obvious. Let's call it the idiot factor. Server based programs bypass you, the technological idiot. You don't have to install or program the filter. More importantly, you don't have to update the filter or even download the updates. Everyday the companies maintain the site. They review the Web and add new inappropriate sites to their list of unavailable areas. Server based filters are much harder for your kids to bypass.

However, there are things that server based programs don't do as well as PC based filtering programs. PC based filters allow the parent to control the time of day the computer is used as well as the amount of private information that the child can release while online.

The best computer protection plan may be a combination of server based and PC based filtering.

Confused? That's ok. Remember I said I was going to walk you through this? I am.

1. Go to your computer.

2. Sit down.

3. Turn it on.

4. Get on the net however you're doing it now.

5. Type in www.filterreview.com. Press enter. Don't be afraid. This site will allow you to pick the level of protection you need. It takes a while to load so be patient.

6. Follow their directions. Several steps later you will have a very well protected computer. You don't have to make the final decision your first visit. You can wait until you and your spouse have researched all the options on this site and then choose . . . Or you can click blindly until you end up filtered.

Filterreview.com is just what it says it is: a review of all the filter providers out there. The site is put together and funded by a group of pro-family nonprofit organizations that want to make it easier for parents to research and choose their own filterware. The founders of the site do not make a profit from the site operation and, of course, I do not make any money by sending you there. (This may be a good time for me to point out that I do not have any financial relationships with any of the organizations or tools listed in this book, with the exception of my own CD and performance descriptions.) With the background I have given you in this chapter and filterreview you will be able to update or choose the filter protection that is right for you.

You can get more information at www.protectkids.com and www.getnetwise.com as well as www.familyclick.com.

Do you really need to do all this? Yes. Moving your computer to a different more easily monitored part of the home may take two hours. Installing and updating filterware may take thirty minutes. OK, two hours if you are technologically illiterate. It's worth the effort.

The Dog Poop Proposal

You will hear it sooner or later. "It's only a little. It's just a small part, *most* of it is good." You may be dealing with a TV show, web site, magazine, movie, song or artist. It doesn't matter. Sooner or latter (probably sooner) you will get the "It's only a little" or "Its only a small part of the whole" excuse.

You are going to be pressed to explain or defend why some music, movies, and books are not acceptable material for your kids to bring into the home or to listen to or see. You need to recognize and respond to the "only a little" strategy when your teen uses it.

It will sound something like this, "Mom, Dad can I go see - *insert movie/song/website/TV show/book name.* Its rated PG-13. It has some of your favorite actors. Even some of our church members said that this movie is good. There is only a suggestion of sex; they never really show it. The Lord's name is only used in vain five times. There is some violence but it's just the regular stuff. It's not really that bad, there are just a few questionable things. There is just a little nudity in the whole thing."

Here is your response. Now, you may have to delay the following activity but you must address the "just a little" protest.

Declare that you are going to have a family baking day. Gather all your teens and bake a family favorite. It can be chocolate chip cookies, whatever. Have each child supervise and contribute to what you are baking. Then take a brief trip outside. Search out and find some dog poop and recover a small bit of it. Scoop it up with a beach shovel and place it into a plastic bag. If you have a family cat or dog this won't present much of an inconvenience for you. Make a trip with your kids to the kitty litter and pick out a cat turd. It doesn't have to be cat or dog but it does have to be some type of excrement. If you live in the city or your neighborhood is devoid of pets then get creative. Go to a pet store and request some poop. Make sure your kids are with you so they know what you produce during the family baking day is the real thing.

You could be the entertainment for your teen

Now go back to the goodie you've been working on and measure off a small amount of the excrement. Mix it into the delicious product you were baking. Dog poop with chocolate cookies works very well. Use a small amount, just a teaspoon.

Your kids will be freaking out and claiming they will never eat what you are creating. You must keep a straight face. Look at them and proclaim, "There is very little dog poop in this batch, it's mostly the same ingredients you enjoy so much. You won't even notice the dog poop. It's only a small part of the ingredients."

Continue to work on the cookies and continue to require them to help. At the same time continue to express puzzlement at their reaction to "just a little dog poop." Bake (or microwave or mix) whatever you decided to create. Offer it to them with this statement, "If you eat all these cookies then you can go to the movie/concert/show that you wanted to go to. You said there was only a little objectionable material in the movie and that it doesn't matter. Well there is only a little dog poop in these cookies, surely it doesn't matter and won't affect you."

You must press this home. Continue to push them to eat the cookie. The reasoning they give not to eat it will be well stated and logical. It is also the same reasoning you can use against the movie. "That dog poop is nasty and it will ruin the whole batch!"

"Well honey, the swearing and suggestive sexual lyrics on that CD ruin the whole c.d."

You can see where I'm going with this. You should have figured it out while I had you picking cat poop out of the kitty litter. Some of you are going to want to bypass the actual exercise and use the logic behind the activity. It's not enough to ask your child, "Would you eat a brownie with a little dog poop in it?" The verbal question does not have the same power as the activity. It will take time, and you may feel the need to throw out a cookie sheet. However you will not have to throw out anything if you employ bleach in the clean up and the point you've made is unforgettable and conclusive. Besides, you know your oven needs cleaning.

If you are hypo-hygienic and the thought of putting excrement inside your oven or microwave is absolutely reprehensible (Even though it can effectively and safely be cleaned), then bake something on a burner. You can throw away the pot!

The violent/sexual movies they want to see are real. The CDs are real. The pornography is real. The illicit sexual material in teen targeted media is *real*. You need *real excrement* in order to prove your point.

By now you may be filled with anxiety. Perhaps you regret picking up this book. You are already busy, pushed to the limit. I have given you so much to do. Now I'm asking you to mess with the computer and you're probably just a little afraid. After all, if took you three days to get it up and running. Your house was thrown into an uproar when you disconnected cable and now I'm asking you to do more.

You're thinking, "All this is laudable, but can I do it?" Yes. Trust your desire to want the best for your child to pull you through.

There is much to distract you. You could be ensnared by the stress you feel. But run with endurance. Fighting for your child's sexual wellbeing is a race against forces that would harm him. Press on.

You gain strength, courage, and confidence by every experience in which you really stop to look fear in the face. You must do the thing which you think you cannot do.
– Eleanor Roosevelt

Action Plan

As a result of reading this chapter what are you going to do and when are you going to do it?

Examples - I will check out www.filterreview.com on Monday then I will sit down and discuss what I have learned with my spouse on _____/_____/_____ .

I will have my children sign the Computer Commandments R.8 on _____/_____/_____ .

I will sit down and see if my computer is protected at all on _____/_____/_____ .

I will ask that guy at work who knows everything about computers how he protects his children. Maybe we can have him over for supper and he can check out our set up.

_____

_____

_____

_____

_____

_____

_____

_____

_____

_____

_____

_____

We must not, in trying to think about how we can make a big difference, ignore the small daily differences we can make which, over time, add up to big differences that we often cannot foresee.
— Marian Wright Edelman

Freedom is always and exclusively freedom for the one who thinks differently.
— Rosa Luxemburg

CHAPTER 9

Monitoring MM Intake (Music & Movies)

We started out chapter seven with some quotes from a few of today's mainstream artists. Let's take a closer look at the music that is out there. You are probably listening to some of the artists listed below and you don't even know it. Can you actually make out the lyrics contained in the music you hear blaring out of Junior's room? Perhaps you're listening to Eminem.

His CD, *The Marshall Mathers LP* contains lyrics that will create objectionable word pictures in your teen's mind. In his song, "Kim" Eminem strangles his wife to death. "Amityville" contains lyrics that describe Eminem chaperoning his sister to a gang rape ("My little sister's birthday. She'll remember me. For a gift I had ten of my boys take her virginity.") Using violence and sex for self-gratification and self-expression is the theme of "Under The Influence." He raps about stabbing people, gunning down children and wants to "smack the preacher while he's preaching."

Within "Criminal" Eminem shares, "if it's not a rapper that I make it as, I'll be a f—ing rapist." In "Kill You" Eminem makes it very clear that he understands the power of music to influence behavior. He screams, "We're...out of our minds and we want in yours. Let us in."

This CD sold 1.7 million copies it's first week and continues to sell millions. His first CD was just as sick. How did the entertainment industry react to his efforts? He won a Grammy and was treated as a hero at the ceremony. What did you expect?

Let me give you another example of what's out there. You may be aware of some of the more prominent death and hate rockers, but it is important you understand the names that you recognize are only the tip of the iceberg. A group called The Bloodhound Gang put out a CD entitled *Hooray for Boobies* that peaked at 14 on the charts. This disk contains songs that sing of a man paying a minor for sex and fantasizing about Jesus sodomizing Mickey Mouse with a lawn dart. The death of Christ is mocked and sex with livestock is promoted.

I don't want to glorify the singular importance of any of the "artists" listed in this book. Certainly a frightened white boy shouting obscenities does not threaten Western civilization. Eminen, Slipknot, and Manson are all insignificant. They will fade away and be replaced with other "artists." It is the thinking and the movement that these artists represent that is a threat. Though the artist themselves are pathetic, the life view they promote should be taken seriously. Sex-saturated teen media is a credible threat to the sexual health of our children.

Don't limit the damage that music can do to what your child is seeing and hearing. Music is their life. It's very important to them - you might even say a religion. The music they listen to influences how they dress, whom they "hang" with, and how they view sex.

You may be reluctant to fight the music battle because it dates you. After all, our parents worried about our music. True. But the music we listened to did not encourage us to rape our sisters, kill our mothers, have sex with animals, and have anal sex with fifteen-year-olds. Some of their music does.

If you rail against their music won't you paint yourself as an out of touch, anti-art, anti-creativity old person? You might as well wear a three-inch wide tie, a polyester suit and a label that reads, "irrelevant." You will not date yourself because you will not yell. There should be no yelling and screaming as a result of this book. (Well maybe a little).

I'm going to show you how to monitor their music without being anti-art, or anti-life. You are going to give them an alternative. You're thinking, "It will never happen." It will, if you keep an open mind about the process. You're not going to wade into your teen's room like Stalin and shout, "No Rock". You are going to calmly let them know they can rock as long as it's clean.

Do you want them to listen to music with a beat that praises death worship and casual sex or music that praises life?

Teens want a beat.

It's your choice.

So your job is simple. Not all of teen music is bad. But some of it is. How do you know? Read the lyrics. Go through Junior's CDs and read the lyrics. Find one of their CDs and open it. If you can't open it have your teen show you how. Take out that funny folded paper and start reading. It should only take you a minute to find out whether that particular CD makes the cut.

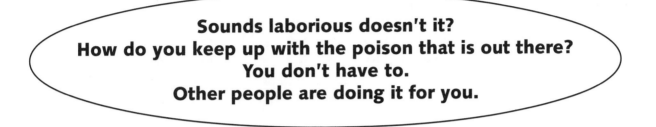

Sounds laborious doesn't it?
How do you keep up with the poison that is out there?
You don't have to.
Other people are doing it for you.

Go to www.screenit.com for music and movie reviews. Use www.ohhla.com to look up the lyrics for specific artists. Neither of these sites has been designed for concerned parents, however, they can serve you. The artists themselves will tell you what they believe in and sing about through their own websites. Simply do a search under the artist's name and then click on "lyrics."

You can find out what groups are blatantly pro-casual sex.

I have proved that this battle is important (remember Hickory Dickory Doc) and several experts support my opinion that music affects behavior and attitude. So here we go....

They want to go to concerts

If you have recently gone through a confrontation you may want to wait a bit before you attack on the music front. In other words, don't take the TV, screen the Internet, pull in their curfew and run the tribe through the wringer all in the same day.

When the time is right, sit them down and explain what you are about to do. Consistency is key. You should be sounding like a broken record by this time. It is important that both parents are present and that you have given yourselves enough time to "do it right." The explanation goes something like this;

but they don't have to go with this dude!

"Some of the music you're listening to can harm you and the way you view life. Because we love you we are going to work together to provide you with music you enjoy and has a positive message. Not everything has to go, so let's look through what you have. We are going to replace each CD we take with a clean alternative. Joey, you are familiar with what you listen to. Joey, what do you think needs to go? Remember, you can buy something just as loud and cutting edge, just so long as the lyrics don't promote sex, drugs, violence or hate. We will drive down to the Book Store and you can listen to some of the samples.

It is important that you do not put down in any way your child's chosen style of music. Throughout the conversation it is important that you continually come back to why you are concerned about what he is listening to. Because you have done your research you can give examples. You may say something like, "Artist "A" makes the statement that he, "hates life" and wants to "kill everybody." Is there any way that can be good for you?" Even though you know you are in control you must do everything possible to make this a joint effort. It will help tremendously if your teen notices that you have taken the time to look up and become familiar with some of his favorite artists.

If at any point during this music exchange either one of you starts yelling, call it off. Come back another day. You need your child's help on this front because music is such a pervasive part of his life. You simply will not be able to monitor everything he buys or listens to at this high intensity level over a long period of time. You need his help. He needs your help. Help each other. He will be relieved to find out that the volume or style is not under attack . . . just the content.

If your child has a large music collection this may be a multi-day process. You can use a combination of processes to dispose of objectionable material.

1. Read the lyrics.

2. Look up a group or artist on one of the web sources I have listed.

3. Print out a list from one of the web sources and compare his collection to the list.

4. Ask your teen to stack up music that must go.

What are the strengths of this strategy?

1. You sat down as a team and explained in a loving manner why you are doing what you are about to do.

2. You did not say all music must go.

3. You did not attack the sound or style of his music. You did not say that rap or metal was bad. You showed you were concerned with content.

4. You gave an alternative.

5. You showed that you are sincere in your concern because the alternative you gave will require your involvement and time. You will have to transport him to the bookstore and continue to monitor his musical choices.

6. You showed your genuine concern because you are going to have to spend money to replace each culled CD.

This is all great, but what about when my child is at another's house or out of my supervision?

During the early teen years "outside your zone" situations are easier to deal with. A twelve-year-old that is not at your house should be at somebody's house. In other words an "early teens" child will usually be under adult supervision even if you are not that adult. Now you have done a great job protecting your child from sex-saturated-media-images at your home. What about their home?

Call them. It's no big deal. You have their names and phone numbers written down in your tribe tracker. Call the host parent and after pleasantries say something like, "My child is not allowed to watch any programming or listen to any music that contains sexual imagery, profanity or violence." Soften it up a bit if you have to, but get the idea across. "That's rude," you're thinking, or, "I'll offend the other parent." I doubt it. And if you do that's too bad.

The reaction you get will probably be positive. The host parent probably wanted to have an in-depth conversation with you but was hesitant because "Nobody does that anymore." By being the first one to come out of the closet you will have opened up clearer communication with someone who should be very important to you, the parents of a tribe member.

What about when they are out with the tribe and outside an adult's supervision? You can't do a thing. At least I'm honest. But you have made a stand in the areas you can control. Once again you are communicating on different levels. Even though your teen may be able to bypass any one of the strategies in the book, you did what you were supposed to do. More importantly, your teen knows you did what you were supposed to do. So even though Friday night might find him sitting in a car while his friend cranks Eminem, he will be thinking about what he is listening to instead of just listening. He may even ask to listen to something else. No, even though you want to believe he will say something like, "That music is against life and against people." He probably won't. He might just say, "I'm tired of that skinny punk. Let's listen to something else." Either way, he's not listening.

So ... this is what a record looks like!

But even if he doesn't do that. He might start to think for himself while he's listening. He might step outside the car mentally and look inside at the ignorant teen consumers. He might start to think for himself. He might step outside the mass herd for just a minute, and think, "There is nothing rebellious about listening to this garbage, everybody does it. The real *individualistic* thing to do is *not* listen to it."

Of course, none of the above
has a chance of happening if <u>you</u> don't make a stand.

We have talked about controlling content (what he listens to). Now lets talk about device control (the thing the music comes through.) With music your options are limited. There are no gizmos available that can be hooked up to his sound system that prevents garbage from coming through. Another challenge associated with music is that it comes through a variety of devices. Garbage can be transported by home stereo, transportable CD player, radio, car radio and tape players, portable headphones, computer, (you can deal with that one with filterware) and TV. The list and the beat goes on. One way to deal with device control is to simply remove the device if you hear or find music that you and the child have agreed to screen out. Draw your line but not in the sand. If that line gets crossed, out comes Junior's sound system.

You should prohibit some groups and artists by name and then use a catchall to describe what you don't want him listening to. It should sound something like this, "Joe, now that we've cleaned out your collection we need to come to an agreement. If I ever hear Manson or Eminem, you're going to lose the system you were listening to. If you play trash through your room system I'll take that. If you're listening to one of your portable gizmos and I discover it's trash you'll lose that gizmo. This "no listen policy" is not limited just to groups we have identified. **If you listen to any music that degrades women, contains foul language, promotes violence, racism and encourages casual sex you will lose your stereo for three weeks.** And remember son, your mother and I love you very much."

Movies present special challenges. Teens often race to be the first to view the new "in" movie. Since we started discussing protecting your child from sex-saturated-media you have noticed a theme or pattern. It's important that you control access to the devices that media come through and control content; Most importantly, you must define what is acceptable. In your adult mind you view all media outlets the same. Teens don't. Your adult mind thinks, "I've set parameters and guidelines for the Internet and TV so he should understand the same expectations hold for Movies and Music." Wrong. Your adult mind may think, "We just finished going through his CD collection yesterday so I don't have to go over what movies are permissible when he goes out tonight." Wrong. Their minds don't work like ours.

You must set expectations and guidelines for each media outlet.

Do not rely on the ratings system to guide you. Another site that can be helpful is www:moviemom.com. This site focuses on movies and strategies to protect your teen from unhealthy viewing. Nell Minow, the creator of the site, can teach you from a mother's perspective. She is also the author of *The Movie Mom's Guide to Family Movies*. (Listed in resource section)

Movies and music represent a large part of the "you aren't cool if you're not having sex message." Divide and conquer. After a while it will become second nature. Just when you are becoming comfortable in your role as guardian of your child's mind you will not have to fill the role. He will have internalized "right thinking" and you can set him free. (Though of course you still have eternal parental nagging rights. But if you want to maintain a healthy relationship with your older non-resident child, I recommend you not use them much.)

Action Plan

As a result of reading this chapter what are you going to do and when are you going to do it?

Examples - Tomorrow I will purchase "The Movie Mom's Gude to Family Movies."

On Saturday we are going to sit down with Billy and have the "music talk." Then we will start going through his collection.

_____

_____

_____

_____

_____

_____

_____

_____

_____

_____

_____

_____

_____

_____

_____

How we spend our days is, of course,
how we spend our lives.
– Annie Dillard

If you bungle raising your children, I don't think
whatever else you do well matters very much.
– Jacqueline Kennedy Onassis

CHAPTER 10

How to Protect Yourself From Resentment and Withdrawal of Affection

At this point you have "intruded" on your child's social life, imposed curfews and limited exposure to teen-targeted-media. You may have even removed a TV from their room or at the very least, disconnected their cable hookup. In short, if you haven't been acting like a parent concerned with your child's sexual worldview, you are beginning to do so. And, if you have not been parenting with authority, you may find yourself at war. You may also find yourself victim of a rather sneaky and usurping parent malady: fear of withdrawal of affection.

We are going to take a break from strategies designed to influence your child's behavior and look at your own behavior. If you are insecure in your love relationship with your child then you will give up on the strategies you've implemented so far and you won't have the courage to continue the struggle.

I know what some of you may be thinking. "If I discipline my child harshly and give up buddy-buddy parenting, won't I alienate him?" I hear this all the time. I also hear, "Won't they resent it when I take their TV, get their friend's phone numbers, monitor their computer and do the things I'm supposed to do?" It is actually a legitimate fear that teens know you have and they will manipulate it to their advantage if you let them. If you have not been doing any of the strategies previously mentioned or coming up, then you need to be ready for attempted alienation.

Parents don't assert themselves because of their own insecurities, not their child's. We must address this, we must answer:

How do you discipline strongly and maintain your love relationship? How do you have input in your child's sexual behavior and maintain a healthy parent relationship? Simple. You balance discipline and guidance with TIME.

The best way to illustrate this idea is with a personal story. When I was seventeen, my parents took my car because I received a D on my report card. My parents said I could keep my driving privileges as long as my grades remained above Cs. This was actually a stretch for me. I was, and this is severely understated, a difficult teen.

He took the car keys!

I was furious. There was no discussion, no battle, and no prolonged plea. They had laid out the parameter and I had crossed it. My parents weren't into appeasement. They were into instruction, and looking back, I'm grateful for it. But I was furious. They pronounced this verdict on a Wednesday, the minute my report card reached their hands.

Actually, Dad made the pronouncement. During my late teen years he was in charge of discipline. To understand my anger you must also know that I bought, insured, and maintained this car with money I earned working part time jobs. My parents didn't buy me the car; I bought it myself. Yet Dad still knocked on the door and asked for my keys. I got a D; I lost the car.

When Dad came for the keys I protested to the point that he threatened to take more privileges and then I handed them over. I hadn't lost my curfew, or my freedom. I had lost my car. That was the deal.

For the rest of the week I was despondent, uncommunicative and basically a sullen jerk. I would not initiate conversations and stayed in my room except for meals. I was using a teen's favorite ploy when confronted with limits: withdrawal of affection.

Your teens may try to use withdrawal of affection in order to get back at you for doing what's best for them. Go figure. They can only use withdrawal of affection if you allow them to.

My parents were the enemy. Only my friends could be trusted.

Do your best to avoid

On Saturday morning my Dad approached my room and pronounced, "Get your skies, we're going skiing."

"I don't want to go skiing," I replied.

"We've had this trip planned for two weeks and we're going."

"That was before you took my car."

"I didn't take your car. You indicated that you did not value your car enough to keep all your grades above a "C." You gave up your own car."

The argument had traveled downstairs and he began to pull his skies off the rack. His motions were short and angry. I protested when he reached for my skis, "I'm not going with you."

"You're going!"

It then became very apparent to my sick, self-involved teen age mind, that I would indeed, be spending a great deal of time with my dad that Saturday.

We loaded the car and we went skiing. We didn't speak on the way to the mountain, but it is impossible not to speak with your skiing partner. I couldn't get myself to hate my Dad for taking my car. I wanted to hate him, as your teenager will momentarily hate you. But I found it impossible to hate him that day. We had a great time together that day, as we always did when we went skiing.

What had he done that day to regain my affection? (Not that I had stopped loving my parents, I had stopped showing that love.) What had he done to restore the relationship? For I was prepared to prolong my siege indefinitely. Had he reiterated his position and reasoning for taking the car? Did he say things like, "Your mother and I took your keys for your own good." No. He indicated that discussion about the car was out of bounds that day. He didn't do any of the above. He simply spent time with me. The type of time that takes planning and effort.

> **The more influence you want on your childs sexual worldview, the more time you must spend with him. Now, I'm trying to keep this book focused on your teens sexual behavior and how you can influence it, but let's face it, much of this is just good parenting.**

All the strategies I'm asking you to implement will meet with varying amounts of resistance and attempted alienation of affection. The less often you have been doing these things up to this time, the more resistance and conflict you will run into.

Studies have shown that buddy-buddy parenting actually weakens the parent child bond and that parenting with authority actually strengthens the parent-child relationship. Researchers discovered, "that despite conventional wisdom that many teens don't want their parents to establish rules and expectations, 47% of teens living in 'hands-on' households reported having an excellent relationship with their fathers and 57% reported having an excellent relationship with their mothers. Only 13% of teens with 'hands-off' parents reported an excellent relationship with their fathers and 24% reported an excellent relationship with their mothers.[1]

Do not be afraid. "Am I to strict?" "Will my child withdraw from me?" And the all time favorite nagging thought, "WILL MY CHILD RESENT ME?" Of course your child will resent you immediately after you take her Eminem CD, move up his curfew, or take pornography away. However, they will not be able to maintain that resentment if you spend time with them, no matter how miserable they try to make you for your efforts.

A book itself can be written on any one of these chapters or strategies. Book after book, study after study, has documented the importance of time. Not quality time, but time. Raw time. Spend it. Let your golf game suffer.

I hear this statement often from parents, "I spend so little time with Jr., I don't feel like punishing him or making him angry with the little time we have." Well, look at the above formula. Parent spends little amount of time, parent feels guilty, and parent does not want to discipline.

Parents themselves admit there is a relationship between the time they spend with children and their feelings about implementing guidance and parameters.

When counseling with families I often have conversations that go like this.

Me - So what have you done as a result of Kevin staying out all night without checking in?

Parent - Well, we talked to him about it.

Me- Were there any actual consequences?

Parent - Not really, His mother and I are working very hard right now and we didn't feel like bringing all that conflict into family time.

Me - So you're not spending as much time together as a family as you would like.

Parent - *Now rather flustered and rather defensive.* No we spend a lot of time together.

Me - Then why do you worry about losing family time to conflict?

Parent - Well, my wife and I don't get home until six o'clock. Sometimes later if the traffic is bad on the way back from getting his sister at daycare. And by the time we eat it's late and we don't really want to argue during that hour or two because that's all we get with them.

Me - What about weekends?

Parent - My wife is taking Saturday classes to get her MBA and I'm coaching his soccer team.

Me - *I know that he plays two games of golf every weekend but I don't mention it because he is already uncomfortable.* So, with the time you have with your children you don't want to fight or argue with your children about grades, curfews, or music choices.

Parent - *Relieved that I now understand this concept and nodding rapidly.* I guess so.

Me - *Gently and in a quiet voice.* So you feel guilty about the lack of time you're spending with your children and don't feel comfortable disciplining them during the little time you have.

Parent - *Now somewhat stricken and conscious of the verbal trap I have sprung, realizing that they themselves have admitted to the above statement.* Well not at all...It's just that we're so busy...and we get so little time. When my wife finishes the MBA program...there's a lot going on at my job...

Me - Are you open to the idea that perhaps you are reluctant to confront inappropriate behavior because you feel guilty about the amount of time you spend with your family?

Parent - Well, it could be possible.

Me - Could we make some changes in priorities that would allow you to spend more time with your children?

Parent - It may be possible...

All over America parents are farming out their kids to schools, daycamp, daycare, and activities. Parents pull up to daycare at seven in the morning so they can get to work by eight. The daycare then busses the children to school. The school then buses the kids back to daycare, and the parents pick the child up from daycare. Children are spending twelve to thirteen hours in the care of others every day. And parents wonder why they are reluctant to discipline.

They say their kids love daycare and that may be true. They say they are comfortable with their choices but deep down they are guilty. And that guilt sometimes manifests itself in reluctance to discipline and set guidelines.

You may not be farming out your child to daycare and para-family organizations. Perhaps your child is older and he comes home to an empty house. The question you must ask yourself is, "Do I spend enough time with my children?" And if you are not you must ask yourself if guilt about spending too little time is affecting your decision-making. You may have put yourself in a position that you have limited contact with your child (after all, you needed that Chevy Suburban).

If you lie awake at night worrying that your children will resent you because you have begun to do what's right, then you have answered the question. If you were spending enough time with your kids, you would not worry about losing their affection.

Now, if you are a dual income family and stressed out, you're going to have to sit down and pick apart your schedule to find additional time for your children so that you will feel comfortable with the strategies I'm asking you to implement.

What is this chapter about? I'm asking you to implement strategies that will anger your child. Some of you will fear that your child will resent you or become estranged from you. You need to battle this fear by spending time with your child.

Remember this formula . . .
TIME = LOVE = CREDIBILITY WITH CHILD

How had my dad kept himself from becoming "the enemy"? Simple. He spent time with me. He spent time with me even though I tried to avoid him. He spent time with me even though I was an unpleasant rebellious, car loser. He spent time with me. He did not allow me to paint him the bad guy.

He did not allow the consequences that I had earned, and he had justly imposed, to stop him from spending time with me.

Parents often ask me, "Won't my child resent me if I limit his curfew, TV time and monitor his dating life? Won't I alienate him if I raid his room and take his drugs, pornography and CDs?" Yes, you will alienate him . . . if you don't spend time with him. You will become a disciplinarian and that is only one role you play as a parent. You must be other things: affirmer, guide, confidant - parent. You can only be these things if you spend time with your teen. Let me make this simple:

**Teens spell love
T.I.M.E**

You spend time. That's it. No matter how bad things got between my parents and me, they always spent time with me and I was unable to villianize them as a result. Now, your teen doesn't want to spend time with you, it doesn't matter, you spend it anyway.

What does this have to do with my child's sexual behavior? Everything. Your child is going to find love somewhere; the need is unmistakable and built in. You can be the provider of love or it could be the boy or girl down the street. You decide.

I'm asking you to discipline and control your teen in order to influence their sexual decision-making. They may rebel. You may be afraid that you are going to "lose them." You will not lose them and they will be unable to shake you if you spend time with them.

It doesn't have to be an outing . . . just simply spend time together

There is no such thing as quality time, there is just time. Many of America's teens are feeling farmed out, bought off, and unloved. You can try to buy them off but it won't work. A TV in their room with the latest equipment and a new car will not replace time. You may feel better but buying them things and taking them on an exotic vacation once a year does not replace love.

If you feel threatened by the chance you may "lose" your child due to your new tougher approach to parenting, spend more time with them. That's it.

Now that you are feeling more confident let's move on to the next strategy. Remember that we are moving from the easiest strategies to implement to the most difficult. Hang on.

What you spend time on says a lot about what you value. Where you spend your time and whom you spend it with says even more about the desires of your heart.

In our society we often say, "time is money." Where do you spend the currency of time? What do you treasure? Men, I know this is a tough one for you. Do you spend the time your kids need or not? Think about it. On his deathbed, no man has ever uttered, "I wish I spent more time at the office."

BRIGHT IDEA . . .

Spend Time
With Your Child

Action Plan

As a result of reading this chapter what are you going to do and when are you going to do it?

Examples - *I'm taking Julie out to eat and to a movie on Friday even though she has been sullen all week and she stayed out after curfew and is grounded.*

I'm going to go Mt. Biking with Julie on _____/_____/_____

_____

_____

_____

_____

_____

_____

_____

_____

_____

_____

_____

_____

_____

_____

CHAPTER 11

The Talk Morphs into the Conversation

You knew it was coming: the talk. You have to do it. Even if you buy your child one of the pro-abstinence books listed in the appendix, you have to talk with them about sex. Even if you ask their therapist to talk with them, *you* have to talk with them. If you truck your teens to a live abstinence rally, you must still sit down and talk with them.

You must talk to your teen about sex.

If you do everything I ask in this book and everything any other pro-abstinence advocate asks, you still must have *the talk*. You have to sit down and talk to your teen about sex, virginity, and intercourse, all of it.

Why? Because you must. By talking with your teenager you back up everything else you're doing to guide them sexually. The talk matters. Your children will respond if they know you are firmly against premarital sex. They have no way of knowing how strongly you feel unless you tell them.

Researchers have documented that:

"The perception by the child that parents disapprove of adolescent sexual activity has consistently been associated with lower rates of sexual activity in youth."[1]

You're going to jump your child with this topic. It may sound sneaky, but if you wait until you feel comfortable, you won't do it. If you wait for the "right opportunity," you won't do it. This needs to be a well-planned and executed attack...err.... talk.

If you're married, you both have to be on board. That's it, period. If you're divorced, call your ex and plan out when you're going to have the talk. Do the best you can to have both parents present. If you are in a blended family then use your judgment. If both biological parents are not on the playing field, then a stepparent can step in. The point is to have the two primary (In the child's view) guardians present.

You pick the time and the place. You should schedule the talk for a time when the teen can't claim a competing event when he discovers the topic. For example, don't schedule the talk for 6:00 if baseball practice is at 7:00. He may decide he has to leave early.

Don't announce early in the day that, "Your mother and I would like to talk to you tonight." He will have all day to build up his non-listening skills and work on his stoneface look.

heads . . . we do the talk today, tails . . . we don't

Have all distractions screened out so that you will be undisturbed. Group three chairs together in a room. Now this may seem extreme, but you need to place yourselves between your child and the room exit. That's right, you have to block flight paths. I've heard reports of kids actually bolting when they discover the topic. Sit side by side for support. Call him or her in and get rolling. How do you start? Anyway you want to.

> ### There is no right way to do this.
> ### The only wrong way to do it is <u>not</u> to do it.

You can start off talking about football as long as you end up talking about sex. I'm going to give you a script. It may take more than one sitting to get through all these topics but that's ok, the talk is going to turn into a conversation anyway.

Following are the topics you must hit during the talk or talks. Go over this several times before you "go in." It is not enough to simply say, "Your father and I don't want you to have sex." You can't simply say, "You could get a disease even if you use protection." You must dig, get specific, and most importantly, get personal.

Not only are you going to discuss the physical dangers of teen sex, you are going to discuss the emotional and psychological consequences of teen sex.

In order to help you create "the talk" each topic will be headed and the following material will be stated in first person. In other words I have converted statistics and complex language into first person dialogue for you. I know that you could do this on your own but I wanted to save you time and take away an excuse for not doing the talk. You may reshape what I have said into your own words. Or you can paraphrase or even go word for word if you want to. After my workshops many parents have told me, "I know what to say, I just don't know how." Well, following you have "what" and "how."

The following assumes that you have introduced the topic and have begun to present your case. At this time your teen may "beg off". Do not allow this to happen. It doesn't matter if she declares she is a virgin and plans to stay that way. It doesn't matter if he says he has been sexually active for years and his girlfriend has been on the pill for years and he has no intention of stopping. If your teen tries to get out of the talk he will use one of two strategies. You may hear, "I am a virgin and plan on staying a virgin, therefore this talk is a waste of time because I agree with you fully and you can't have anything to add to my infinite wisdom and reasoning." Or you may hear, "I have been sexually active, am sexually active, we are using protection. I can handle it and you can't have anything to add to my infinite reasoning and wisdom."

You do have something to add to their infinite reasoning and wisdom.

Let's look at some ways you can counter their attempt at dodging.

TFD - (Remember, Teenager Feigning Disinterest) Mom, I know how you and Dad feel about this and I agree with you. I'm not going to have sex until I'm married, so can I go now?

YOU - Sweetheart, you can't know exactly how we feel because we have never talked about this in depth. There is more to our reasoning than, "Don't have sex". We are happy that you are delaying sex, however, that does not make what we have to say today unimportant. Please sit down.

OR

TFD - Mom, Dad, I don't really think you have a right to tell me how to behave sexually. I have been sexually active so you're a little late. We are using protection and we are handling it, so can I go now?

YOU - Son, you're right, if you insist on having sex we can't stop you. However, we are not too late. As your parents we have a right to tell you how we feel. This is not just going to be a "you may catch a disease or get her pregnant" talk. There are emotional and spiritual dangers that we don't think you are considering.

OR

TFD - Oh please, I know all about this stuff. I know all about protection and failure rates and I'm old enough to deal with sex. We have dealt with this at health class in school.

YOU - I hear you saying that you don't need this talk, and you may not *(even though you believe they do)* but we want you to listen. We think we have some ideas that may surprise you. This isn't going to be a simple 'Don't have sex' talk. We have special "inside information" for you.

Do you see how you get them to sit down if they use one of the above three resistance strategies? You agree with them. If your son tells you he is a virgin and plans on staying one don't tell him you don't believe him or don't trust his commitment. If you daughter tries to tell you that she is sexually active and that makes what you are about to say irrelevant, don't attack her sexual activity. Do attack the idea that what you have to say does not matter.

Don't attack, do disarm. Don't be thrown off track. This is not a time to talk about respect or "how to address your parents." In this instance you must be ready to take some abuse in order to get your message out.

Bud's response to his son's admission of sexual activity

For some of you none of the above will be necessary. Your teen may compliantly slouch into a chair and prepare himself for the talk. Your teen may even welcome the discussion even though he will do everything possible to lead you to believe you are stupid and irrelevant. No matter what type of body language he uses to tell you he is not listening, believe me, he is listening.

Ok, now we have him seated and pretending not to listen, let's get going. Remember that I've broken this talk into sections so you can divide it up. Dad may take one and three while mom takes two and four and so on. I will be using male and female pronouns to give you an idea of the sound and tone. It is important that you are not derogatory. One of the reasons that I'm including the script is that many parents convey the right information in the wrong way. Try to keep an air of respect around this conversation. Do not talk down or belittle. This is one time you may want to give a little ground as far as what you will tolerate. In other words, if they act disrespectful, ignore and press on in a conciliatory tone.

Use the same script for sons or daughters. Just do this one person at a time. For example, If you have two sons who are fourteen and sixteen don't try to address them both in the same sitting. You lose the impact and they will not open up in front of each other. Remember this is a unisex script; modify it to fit your situation and remember to flip flop gender as the need arises. You may want to take notes from this. You won't need more than a sheet. Just scratch down what you think are the teaching points from each section and rephrase them in your own words. Then you will have a personalized outline.

I have not included your teen's probable response because I don't know what it will be. Some teens will nod their head and say nothing. This is bad. You want a response even if you don't like what you hear. Do everything you can to make this a conversation rather than a lecture. Ask questions and listen. The following looks like a lecture because I have written your lines, not his. Do everything you can to get him talking about his fears and what is happening in his/her life.

The Talk - One
Bad stuff can still happen even though you may be/are-using protection.

Son, Your mother and I know that you can buy condoms at Wal-Mart or even get other birth control devices downtown at the clinic. But we just want you to know that all those things have failure rates. Condoms fail ten to thirty percent of the time because they slip off, break, or leak. Now son, we do admit that condoms do reduce the risk of disease or pregnancy. But is "reduce" good enough for you? We think you're better than that. Studies have shown that condoms have up to a thirty percent failure rate in preventing the transmission of the AIDS virus.

One third of sexually active teenage girls have either human papilloma virus or chlamydia. Both of these diseases can be spread by skin to skin contact between genital areas. A condom only covers the penis and does not protect the whole genital area.

The Talk - Two
Why worry when you could be happy with abstinence?

Sweetheart, you have enough to worry about. You may not realize it now but sexual involve-ment will give you more garbage to deal with at a time when you just don't need it. Do you want to be lying awake at night wondering if you're pregnant or have a sexual disease? You know how concerned you get about some things. Just remember how worried you were about your exams last semester. You couldn't eat and thought about it all the time. Now think for a moment. The exams were important, but nowhere near as important as pregnancy or a disease would be. Imagine how much you would worry about those things

I'm not wishing worry on you. And I'm not saying that if you have sex you will get pregnant or catch a disease. I do know even if you don't, you will worry about it.

The Talk - Three
You can run but you can't hide, guilt will find you.

Sweetheart, once it's done it's done, and you can not undo it. Let's face it, you are probably not going to spend your life with your teen sexual partner. That means the relationship will end. You will have given a part of yourself to someone who does not care about you. That will hurt. You may have sex because you feel that it will lead to love. But chances are that he was not that emotionally committed and he was more interested in the sex. You may feel guilty or used when the relationship ends. (If talking to a girl at this time it is important for dad to explain that yes, boys are capable, as are men, of feigning affection in order to get sex). Sweetheart, we don't want you to get hurt and be burdened with guilt. Premature sex often happens between the user and the used. We don't want you to be either.

Son, I know you are very interested in sex. But at what price? What if you get sexually involved with a girl? To her that sex will mean something different than it will to you. She will believe you love or care about her deeply. Will you? When the relationship ends, do you want to be the one responsible for all that pain? You know how your mother and I feel about this issue. Yes it's true we can't follow you around and prevent you from becoming sexually involved. But you know how we feel. Do you want to bring that kind of guilt into our relationship as a family? We are at odds about enough, do we need this?

The Talk - Four
You don't want to have to pay for therapy, do you?

Son, sex is powerful. Sex adds weight to an experience. It makes everything in an experience "heavy." If you enter into a sexual relationship you may risk your long-term emotional health. If you get hurt in a sexual relationship it could affect the way you view women. As we said earlier, you may be exploited for sex. You may not trust anyone after that.

Sweetheart, we want you to have a wonderful sex life when you get married. Sex too early can ruin how you feel about sex for a lifetime. You may never trust a man fully if you are used. We don't want that for you. If one guy uses you for sex you may feel that that's all men really want. You may block out the man that truly loves you because of an extremely painful event that occurred earlier.

Son, sometime during your teenaged career you will get dumped. It happens to everyone. A girl will end a relationship with you. It will hurt. Now get this; it will hurt much more if you were sexually active within that relationship. Adding sex to a relationship changes that relationship. It can lead you to believe that there is a strong commitment in the relationship, that you are loved. And when that relationship ends you will suffer even more if it was sexual.

The Talk - Five
Don't get out of focus

Sweetheart, the interests, hobbies, friendships and activities you participate in now will effect you the rest of your life. Sex too soon will pull you away from what is truly good for you. Sexual activity outside of marriage can be distracting and demeaning. Dating relationships that include sex are almost always obsessive and overpowering. Do you know what we mean son? There is so much opportunity in your life now. You shouldn't waste the time and resources that you now have on a sexual relationship that will not last. You will never have more time and opportunity around you than you do now. I know you think you are busy, but you will look back when you are older and realize how good you had it.

Son, we don't think that sex is bad and we are not anti-sex. We are just anti-sex outside of marriage. Sex is a wonderful thing. It is both powerful and pleasurable. And like many things that give emotional and physical pleasure, it can be all you think about once you get started. Remember that run we took at the mountain last year, the expert trail you almost killed me on? You were so excited. You looked ecstatic as you snowboarded down that thing. As soon as you got to the bottom you headed for the lift. I had to drag you off the slopes that day, and all week long you bugged me to go back. Now you talk, walk, and eat snowboarding. It makes you feel good. You have a healthy obsession with snowboarding. There's nothing wrong with it. However, you could develop a very unhealthy obsession with sex. You see snowboarding is a sport, while sex is a very strong *desire*. What if I told you there would be no snowboarding allowed from now on? You would be upset wouldn't you? Now, sex would be an even greater obsession if you got involved with it. What happens when that relationship ends? You would hurt, wouldn't you? It's not just the risk of hurt we are worried about.

The obsession with sex itself is dangerous. If you become obsessed with sex you may lose interest in the things around you that you used to enjoy. Son, you're only a teenager once. You have more time in your life than you will ever have again. I know this is hard for you to understand. Even if you escape from a sexual relationship without a disease, pregnancy, or emotional pain, harm was still done if you missed out on the opportunities of your teen years because of your obsession with a sexual relationship. Now is the time to develop yourself. There will be time for sex later. Your teen years are brief and so are the opportunities that come with them.

After you complete the above (in one or more sittings) you can't simply check off the talk. You must keep the lines open. This topic must periodically come up.

Remember, this is a *conversation*. It goes on after the talk. The talk morphs into an ongoing dialogue about sex. How does this happen? It happens because you yourself have changed the way that you think about sex. You now see yourself as the primary sexual model for your children. You understand that sexual instruction is part of your job description, and because this responsibility is on your mind you look for opportunities to teach and share.

The talk should be the start of an ongoing conversation. Research backs this up; "The data suggest that just talking about sex with children is not enough; parents must make a definite effort to convey their values and expectations about sexual activity to adolescents and to 'connect' with them. Communicating values and expectations and 'connecting' involves <u>more than just one or two discussions.</u> Rather, this communication will require modeling by parents and frequent repetition." [2] (underline mine)

How the talk morphs into the conversation

All you have to do is look for an "in." An "in" is anything that can bring up the topic or serve as an illustration. Once you use an "in" does not mean it's used up. You can use different prompts or "ins" as much as you want. Following are some examples of how the talk morphs into a periodic conversation:

The Pledge Certificate and Ring Event

A few days after you have the talk ask your son/daughter if they would like to sign a pledge certificate and/or receive a promise ring. Reproduce (on quality paper that matches your child's room) the pledge certificate on page R.15 in Appendix B. Have him/her sign it, witness it, and frame it. There should be a degree of ceremony attached to this. Then present a promise ring (they can be ordered from www.lifeway.com/tlw/) to him or her. This ring is worn on the wedding finger and is a physical symbol of the wearer's commitment to wait until marriage. They come in different sizes and styles and inscribed with different pro abstinence symbols and words. The meaning of these rings is recognized within youth culture.

The Billboard

You're driving down the highway and notice a billboard for *Hooters,* which of course, features some very disproportionate ladies. You point to it and say something like, "Son do you really think people go there for the chicken? How is sexual desire and imagery being used to sell a product?" You and your son then talk about how sex is used in advertising, which leads to a discussion on how sex is portrayed in the media. He then starts talking about how sex is so commonplace at his high school. This conversation leads to his admitting how he has felt pressured to be sexually active. This leads to his description of the sexual situations he has had to deal with. (Perhaps successfully or unsuccessfully) You then give advice and reassure that abstinence is the way to go and that, "Real men wait."

This whole conversation lasts an hour and covers a lot of emotional ground. All because you made a comment about a billboard. All because you took the time to talk. All because you took seriously your responsibility to influence your child's sexual worldview.

The Bills (Finances)

You're sitting down going through your bills. You call your son over and motion to the pile. "Son, I want you to run the calculator and total those up for me. Then call out each balance due on each bill as I write out the checks" This goes on for twenty minutes. (If you were in my house it would go on for two hours.) At the end of this exercise you look at your son and say something like, "It costs a lot more than you thought to run a house doesn't it?" You and your son discuss different bills. You can then go into the costs of a baby or raising a family. Or perhaps you could use the bills to talk about life and being a real man. You could say something like, "Son, sex is easy, supporting your family and meeting your responsibilities takes a man."

Clothing

You're sitting at the mall while shopping with your daughter. A teenage girl strolls by "working it". She is wearing a skintight tanktop, with a painful push up bra, tight pants and four-inch heals. You nod to your daughter and ask, "What message is she broadcasting?" Don't be surprised if the answer you get is not the one you want. Your daughter may say, "There isn't anything wrong with what she's wearing." You then go into how men are visual creatures and how they are stimulated visually. You use the clothing as an "in" to other topics.

Diaper Duty

Volunteer for the nursery at a church, civic function, or watch the baby of a relative and have your teenager do duty with you. Make it a fine mother-daughter or father-son adventure. Have your little sweetie change the stinkiest, nastiest diaper of the morning. When she recovers you may want to say something like; "They don't show diaper changing on MTV do they. Sex leads to babies and if you're not ready to change diapers at three in the morning then you're not ready for sex." You may go on to a real definition of love. Something like, "Love is patient, love is kind, love bears ill will and changes diapers."

End Positive

You get the idea. You use an event or image to bring up the topic. Whatever you do, end positive, even if it hurts. Remember the culture of their world paints parents as anti-sex and anti-fun. Do not contribute to this. Make a positive statement about our plan for sex. You could say something like; "Your mother and I want you to have a fulfilling sex life within marriage, which is why we're having this conversation." Or perhaps you could end with, "Sex can be such a wonderful part of your married life, we just don't want you to blow it." Or "Son don't get me wrong. Sex is a wonderful thing; we just want it to be wonderful for you within marriage."

> **Every time you talk with your teen about sex, and I mean every time, you end positive about sex.**

Purchase or order some of the tools listed in the back of the book. Put in a CD that features an abstinence message and rock all the way to the beach. Get one of the abstinence calendars or abstinence posters. Comment on the quote or lyrics.

You get the idea. Opportunities to talk about sex are endless (thanks to a sex saturated society) You just have to take advantage of them to create an "in." Once you get "in" don't lecture. Listen . . . and talk.

Action Plan

As a result of reading this chapter what are you going to do and when are you going to do it?

Examples - *I will sit down with my spouse and plan the talk on* ____/____/____

I will check with my son to see what his schedule is.

I will arrange to have the other kids out of the house on ____/____/____

_____

_____

_____

_____

_____

_____

_____

_____

_____

_____

_____

_____

_____

_____

_____

_____

CHAPTER 12

Sex Isn't Supposed to Kill You!

Sexually Transmitted Diseases, Oral Sex, and Your Child

I n this chapter you are going to learn how to use the <u>reality</u> of sexually transmitted diseases to prevent your child from <u>getting</u> sexually transmitted diseases (STDs). You will learn the truth about the carnage that is occurring "out there" and then be able to graphically educate your child using R.13 and R.14 from Appendix B. Before you educate your child, you must educate yourself.

There is an epidemic of sexually transmitted diseases amongst teens occurring as you read this. Yet, nowhere in teen culture is the perception of danger so out of touch with reality. How bad is it? Let's look at some facts.

Everyday, 8,000 teens will become infected with a new STD. [1]

10% of teenage girls have chlamydia. Half of new chlamydia cases occur in girls 15 to 19 years old. [2]

Nearly 50% of African-American teenagers have genital herpes.[3]

One in five children over age 12 tests positive for herpes type 2. [4]

You read that right. One in five children age twelve and over have herpes. Let me say it again. One out of five teens have an incurable virus. Want me to say it again? Let me elaborate. Does your son or daughter have ten friends in their tribe? Two of them have herpes. I know what you're thinking, not these kids, not this neighborhood. Diseases do not discriminate. Reread chapter one. Socioeconomic factors do not protect your teen against premarital sex or the disease that comes with it.

Go to the mall, a football game, country club, or wherever. If you see a group of teens hanging around, several of them will have a sexually transmitted disease. How can I be so sure? Because statistic after statistic and study after study show that the national STD epidemic has permeated all American demographic groups. There is no way your community is immune. No way.

Why is this? Why do so many teens have herpes or human papilloma virus (HPV)? Because there are four myths that are deeply embedded in teen culture. They are complete and utter falsehoods that many teens except as fact:

The Four Myths

1. STDs are rare at my school and within my tribe.

2. Oral sex is not sex and you cannot get a disease from oral sex.

3. Condoms are effective against disease.

4. Adopting an A.B.I. (Anything But Intercourse) approach to sex will keep me safe from diseases.

What They Believe

The "four myths" are powerfully imbedded within the psyche of the nation's youth. This is not just my opinion. What I'm calling "The Four Myths" has been substantiated by studies conducted by a variety of public and private agencies.

Many teens refer to oral sex and mutual masturbation as "abstinence."[5]

Six out of ten teens believe that oral sex is not sex and two out of ten believe that anal sex is not sex.[6]

Out of a pool of 10,000, eight out of ten girls said they were virgins, even though one-fourth of the "virgins" had had oral sex. Over half the respondents (5,700) were under 14 years old.[7]

Safe Sex and the Condom Crises

There are two forces at work here: the fallout from "safe sex" (condom promotion) propaganda and the fallout from the sex scandals of the nineties. Safe sex was, and still is, the mantra of many organizations. A former president argued, "oral sex is not sex." The combination of the safe sex push and the insistence by this individual and his apologists that oral sex was not sex had a disastrous effect on the nation's youth.

Because they believe the four myths, many teens have bought the idea that condoms will keep them safe. There is just one little problem: condoms are completely ineffective in preventing the transmission of the herpes, HPV and chlamydia. You see, these three diseases can be spread through skin-to-skin contact. Condoms are a barrier method to prevent an exchange of fluids. Therefore they do *reduce* the chance of HIV transmission and pregnancy because both these events require the transmission of fluids. However, herpes, HPV and chlamydia do not need an exchange of fluids to take place in order to be contracted. The condom only covers the penis, not the whole genital area. Therefore, when wet, moist genital areas come into contact, the viruses and bacteria can be spread.

Herpes can also be spread through oral sex. Didn't know this? I'm not surprised. Does your teen know this? Does he know that he can get herpes through genital contact even if he uses a condom? Does he know that he can get herpes from oral sex or "outer course?" I doubt it. If your school is still a "Safe Sex" or "Comprehensive Ed" school then I doubt he knows it. You see, the safe sex and condom crowd is doing everything they can to suppress this information. I repeat: those that distribute and promote condoms do not educate people about their products proven ineffectiveness against herpes, chlamydia, and HPV. Why? "Safe Sex" education and condom distribution are big businesses. You do the math. The facts show that condoms have a large failure rate against certain diseases. It's up to you to educate your child to the facts. I'm going to give you a way to do this. But first I want to give you a better understanding of "the myths" and the science of STD transmission.

Teens view condoms as a solution. They are ignorant of the facts surrounding condoms, namely, the fact they do not protect against diseases. This is not their fault, it is ours. When I say "ours," I mean the adults of America. You see, they don't think of us as safe sex advocates or abstinence advocates, Republicans or Democrats, Liberals or Conservatives. We are just "them." And the dominant message, on any topic, is attributed to "us," the adults. They were told to practice "safe sex." Safe sex was then defined as sex while using a condom. The word "safe" implies complete protection, not *partial* protection. When a runner is called "safe" in baseball that runner is not partially safe, he is completely safe. You can see how young minds were misled by the "safe sex" message. When condom advocates suffered the fallout from condom failure they changed the language to "protected sex." Once again, this is misleading. The young person then thinks, "I'm using a condom, I'm protected." Protected from what? Condoms have been shown to be ineffective against diseases such as herpes and HPV. Does that mean protection?

Your adult mind thinks, "How can teens believe that condoms would assure them *complete* protection from disease and pregnancy, surely they must know that there is still some risk?" Your adult mind is wrong. They trust condoms because we have told them to for years, because MTV promotes them, because we used words like "safe" and "protected" when describing them, and because they want them to be to be 100% effective.

Let's look at some facts:

While condoms have been shown to reduce transmission of HIV/AIDs, there is not enough evidence to determine that they were effective in reducing the risk of most other sexually transmitted disease. [8]

**When used properly 100% of the time, condoms reduce the risk of gonorrhea transmission by 50%.
Or stated simply, condoms have a 50% failure rate against gonorrhea.[9]**

Condoms have no impact on the risk of sexual transmission of human papilloma virus (HPV) in women. And there is no clear evidence that condoms reduce HPV transmission in men. [10]

Using condoms does not help men reduce the risk of getting herpes. [11]

There is a fact, a fact that you will repeat over and over again until your teen becomes an adult, and a fact that you will emphasize during the "Myth Bashing" exercise in the appendix. This fact requires you use honest language and not skirt the issues. What is that fact? Simply this:

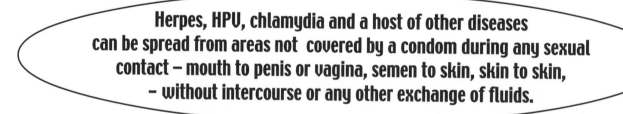

Herpes, HPV, chlamydia and a host of other diseases can be spread from areas not covered by a condom during any sexual contact – mouth to penis or vagina, semen to skin, skin to skin, – without intercourse or any other exchange of fluids.

Why is the above fact so important? Because it destroys three of the "four myths." It is impossible to hold two opposing viewpoints at one time. Can your teen believe that oral sex is safe and believe that many diseases can be spread through oral sex? Can your child believe that condoms offer complete protection when he also believes that herpes can be spread through skin-to-skin contact? Can your child believe that engaging in sexual contact while avoiding penetration and ejaculation will keep him safe when he believes that diseases can be spread through a variety of surfaces and activities? The answer is "no!" This is what I mean by using disease to prevent disease. Now that we have exposed the lie of "safe sex" let's take a look at the effect of the "oral sex is not sex" lie on teen behavior.

The oral sex craze was probably inevitable because teens are in a centuries old search for pleasure that avoids consequences. However, our former president's insistence that "oral sex is not sex" certainly didn't help things. Long after that sentence saturated the airwaves, the skewed logic it conveyed was filtering into teen culture.

I have a line in my comedy show that I'll share here:

> ## Oral sex is sex! That's why the word "sex" is after "oral!"

I first became aware of the increase of oral sex in the teen and preteen population through anecdotal evidence; stories of teens caught on the bus performing oral sex and stories of herpes outbreaks in groups of teens that had not had intercourse. I didn't want to believe what distraught teachers and parents were telling me. However, a few years after this trend emerged on the front lines it was being verified by credible studies conducted by a variety of agencies.

Of 1,067 teens aged 13 to 18 surveyed in the early 1980s, roughly one-fifth (20%) said they had participated in oral sex. But ten years later, that figure had jumped to 70% of males and 57% of females. [12]

26% of sexually active 15-17 year olds surveyed said one "cannot become infected with HIV by having unprotected oral sex" and an additional 15% were unsure. [13]

The majority of teens questioned did not believe that oral sex qualified as sex and were unaware that HIV, herpes, syphilis, gonorrhea, HPV, chancroid, intestinal parasites, and Hepatitis A can be contracted during oral sex.[14]

When you think about it, this phenomenon makes perfect sense. The leader of the free world declared that, "oral sex is not true sex." His legal council and assorted media defendants elaborated that it wasn't sex "unless penetration and ejaculation occurred." These messages reverberated within teen culture. Adults understood *why* he was making such an absurd statement. Most teens *at the time* understood. Eight and nine year olds did not. Because of their limited ability to think analytically, they accepted what they heard as fact. Those kids are teens now. Children who don't even remember our former president now believe that "oral sex is not sex." They don't know where they got the belief. They just believe it. Like all cultural changes, the idea that "oral sex is not sex" seeped into teen culture. Who knows how the idea that coolness is connected to piercing your tongue or navel spread? Those ideas and behaviors just became part of teen culture while we were out for coffee. Much like any other teen fad, the idea that "oral sex is safe and not 'real' sex" spread. Oral sex has become the new fashion statement. We can't blame the children, they just processed the information and came to their own conclusions: *Oral sex is not real sex, therefore I can tell my parents I'm not having sex and still meet my boyfriend's physical needs with oral sex. Since oral sex is not "sex," then I will be safe from "sexually" transmitted diseases if I engage in oral sex.*

The appeal of oral sex for young people is obvious: pregnancy is avoided. Pregnancy *is* avoided but diseases are not. Teens worry about pregnancy more than disease because pregnancy can be seen and "talked about." From the teen's perspective, pregnancy more obviously changes the direction of his/her life. In their minds oral sex offers the pleasure of sexual contact without the risk. *You* have to convince them otherwise.

The point here is that you must get your child to give up the four myths and believe the truth. This will be harder than simply *telling* him the truth. I cannot emphasize enough how embedded the four myths are in youth culture. If your teen has bought into one of the four myths, then be prepared for his initial reaction to the facts to be disbelief rather than acceptance. He may even believe that you have made up "the facts" in order to scare him out of having sex. There is no need for you to make up anything because the truth is frightening enough.

You may be wondering why I didn't include this "disease" component in "the talk." The answer is rather complex and has to do with learning theory. In a nutshell, you wanted a broad conversation when you had "the talk." You were not specifically taking on four medically related "ideas." Also, what you were saying was not as difficult for your teen to believe as what you are about to say. For example, when you had "the talk," it may have made sense to your teen that "he could get emotionally hurt by experimenting with sex." He may have already felt some pain. However, if your teen has been indoctrinated into believing that oral sex is safe, it will be difficult for him to accept that it is not. You see, in his mind you may have *some* credibility when talking about concepts such as "hurt" and "his future." But you have *no* credibility when talking about oral sex and disease. Therefore, you will have to show him the research and graphically explain why you believe what you believe. He will then be *forced* to process the information.

This may seem dramatic, but I can't emphasize this enough. Simply *telling* your teen that condoms have been shown to be ineffective against chlamydia will have very little impact on his belief if he has accepted and nurtured the lie that condoms will protect him. Defeating the "four myths" will be made more difficult depending on the length of time your teen has believed in and nurtured a particular myth. Because of the way the mind works, a tenth grader will be much more indoctrinated in the "oral sex = safety" myth than a seventh grader. In these examples we are assuming that your teen strongly believes the "four myths." If you feel he does not, great, still do the exercise. Remember, there is power in seeing a scientific idea in print. There is even more power in having your child go on the web and see this information in print. There is behavior-changing power in getting your child to read these facts and have them "sign off" that they understand them.

Let's Go Myth Bashing!

Following is an example of what to say and do while you're leading them through the "Myth Bashing" exercise in R.13 and R.14. Please do not skip this exercise.

When you change something on a monetary check you initial it and sign off. When you bought your house, you read all the clauses and signed off. You were made to understand that if you did not make your payments there would be consequences. When you make any major commitment you are asked to acknowledge something in print and sign off. The closing attorney did not tell you that you would lose your house if you failed to pay your mortgage. He had you *read* and *sign* a statement that said so.

Teens are beginning to enter a world where they must "read and sign." They had to get their field trip permission slip signed. They had to sign their driver's license application and they had to sign paperwork in order to take the SAT. They were made to understand the consequences of cheating and they signed. In this exercise they will acknowledge and sign facts that pertain to their very lives.

Each of the four myths is listed. Underneath are statements that contradict the myth (labeled truth). Underneath the truth statements you will find the research (labeled evidence) that support the argument against the myth. Following the evidence you will find the researching organization. (Notice none of the organizations are listed as "hysterical sex hating parents.") The rules are the same as they were for "the talk." When you meet with your teen your spouse must be present. Do not let them beg off or put you off (either teen or spouse). Make this a surprise visit or "pounce." Ideally, your teen should read you the whole "Myth Bashing" exercise. This may be a hard sell. If you can't get him to read all the statements aloud then push to have him read the research statements aloud. It is very important that your child read aloud the research (evidence) statements!

Below is an example of one "cycle" of the "Myth Busters" exercise. As you will see there is a rather Socratic progression. First you introduce the myth. You may introduce it by asking, "Do condoms keep you safe from sexually transmitted diseases?" Then you read or have him read the truth. See if he can restate the truth in his own words. You may ask him, "What does that mean? "Why does it matter that condoms don't cover all genital areas that come into contact?" Don't feel comfortable asking such graphic questions? Tough.

Myth: Condoms Protect against Disease

Truth

Condom protection is most effective against pregnancy (10 -15% failure rate when used properly *all* the time) The failure rate of condoms against Sexually Transmitted Diseases varies from 30% to no measurable prevention affect at all. Besides the risks that fluid may be exchanged through slippage, perforation, and small holes, there remains the risk of infection from contact of areas not covered by a condom. Diseases such as herpes, HPV and chlamydia can exist on the _area surrounding the base of the penis on a man and the vagina of a woman._ This means there is opportunity to contract an STD _while properly using a condom._ Condoms are not effective against disease because they only cover the head and shaft of the penis.

Evidence

Condoms have no impact on the risk of sexual transmission of human papilloma virus in women. And there is no clear evidence that condoms reduce HPV transmission in men. "Federal Panel on Condoms Offers Crucial Warnings to Sexually Active Americans, Says The Medical Institute for Sexual Health" NIH Condom Report Release. The Medical Institute for Sexual Health, July 19, 2001 _____ **Initial**

The power of the exercise is having your child read the evidence aloud. Make sure he understands why the evidence is important. As an example, with the above evidence statement you might say, "You see Joey, they can't find solid evidence that shows condoms work well against _all_ sexually transmitted diseases. These people are not crazy parents, they are scientists."

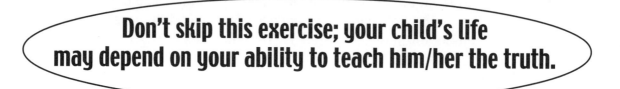

Don't skip this exercise; your child's life may depend on your ability to teach him/her the truth.

Ok, go to the back of the book and make copies of R.13 and R.14. Take some prep time, and go for it. Remember, it's up to you to tell your child the truth about the four myths!

Action Plan

As a result of reading this chapter what are you going to do and when are you going to do it?

Examples – I will study the Myth Bashing exercise on _____/_____/_____.

I will meet with my child and go through R.13 and R.14 on _____/_____/_____.

I will call my ex-husband to see if he will "do chapter 12" on ____/____/____

_____

_____

_____

_____

_____

_____

_____

_____

_____

_____

_____

_____

_____

_____

**Of all the hard things to bear and grin,
the hardest is being taken in.**
– Phoebe Cary

**The failure of public health efforts to prevent
the STD epidemic in America is related to the
CDC's "safe-sex" promotion and its attempts to
withhold from the American people the truth
of condom ineffectiveness.**
– Physician Groups and Politicians calling for the resignation
of the head of the CDC, July 25, 2001 HIV/AIDS Report

CHAPTER 13

The Power of Daddy Love

I have seen more tears in my adult audience when talking about the father-daughter relationship and its effect on sexual behavior. More women have approached me after the workshop about this topic then any other in this book. If you had no relationship with your father or no father while you were growing up, I'm sorry for the pain that may follow. However, we must cover this ground.

What is the biggest statistical indicator for teen-age female sexual activity? What situation puts a girl at risk more than any other? What is more dangerous than drugs or violence to a teen-age girl's sexual well being? Answer: growing up without feeling the love and acceptance of a father.

The Centers for Disease Control and Prevention surveyed 4000 youths from age 12 to 21. They discovered those female adolescents from mother-only families were nearly twice as likely to report having had sexual intercourse than peers in intact families.[1]

Girls who live absent of their biological fathers, on average, are more likely to be poor, experience educational, health, emotional and psychological problems, be victims of child abuse, be sexually active, and engage in criminal behavior than their peers who live with their married biological mother and father.[2]

Studies that show the relationship between father absence and teen pregnancies abound. I will spare you the redundancy. Just understand this: organizations from all over the political spectrum have sponsored studies and they all show basically the same thing. They often disagree on why or by what percentage, but the connection is always there. The absence of a father increases the risk of teen pregnancies from one hundred and fifty percent to two hundred and fifty percent. These studies consistently show that girls without contact with a father are one and a half to two and half times more likely to become pregnant outside of marriage during their teen years.

Research that shows a link between the father relationship and the sexual behavior of girls is very specific. A positive father daughter relationship has been shown to delay the onset of puberty and (once again) sexual intercourse. Delay puberty? Exactly. Researchers tried to isolate the factors that delay the beginning of pubertal development in girls. What was the most dominant factor? The presence of a warm, attentive, biological father in the home. The report summarizes that, "The quality of father's investment in the family emerged as the most important feature of the proximal family environment relative to daughters' pubertal timing."

If it seems that girls enter puberty sooner to you, you're right. If it seems that there are eleven-year-old girls that look like they should be in twelfth grade, it's not you, you're right. These researchers wanted to find out why some girls are menstruating at ten years of age and others at fifteen. The researchers discuss the social implications of the data; "early pubertal maturation, risky sexual behavior, and early age of first birth are all components of an integrated reproductive strategy that derives in part, from low paternal investment."[3] If you will allow me to translate the above for you; early puberty increases the risk of early promiscuous sexual behavior and teen pregnancy.

This is a rare case when "Delay" is something you actually want. Why? Is it healthy for an eleven-year-old to have the capability to reproduce? Do you really want to deal with an eleven-year-old that would make Brittany Spears proportionally envious? Do you want your daughter to have to deal with the attention her curves will garner from boys six and seven years older? A strong relationship with Dad will push puberty back to where it is supposed to be. You were probably aware to some degree, that the father-daughter relationship had an effect on teen pregnancies. Now you know that this relationship is so pivotal to a young girl's sexual well being that it can even influence the beginning of puberty.

And something even more alarming has risen from social research. Girls in a dysfunctional relationship with their fathers are at the same level of risk as girls with no contact or with no father figure at all. So, if dad is in the house but does not have a loving relationship with his daughter he is doing as much harm as if he were not there at all.

These researchers looked at the intensity and quality of father-child dialogue. They found that,

"Children who feel a closeness to their <u>father</u> are twice as likely as those who do not to enter college, to find stable employment after high school, <u>75 percent less likely to have a teen birth,</u> 80 percent less likely to spend time in jail, and half as likely to experience multiple depression symptoms."[4]

Girls need to know that Dad loves them. They need to feel the special approval of their father. They need "Daddy Love." Why haven't you been hearing more about these studies? Well, what could be more politically incorrect than announcing that girls need their fathers?

A girl who does not feel love from a father figure will search for "love" with another male figure. If Dad does not give her love and approval perhaps the boy down the street will.

Why the connection between fatherhood and teen female sexual behavior? This is a practical book on strategy and I don't want to spend (nor am I able) the time necessary to give a complete explanation of this social phenomenon. But we must try to understand the connection between lack of "Daddy Love" and the sexual behavior of teen girls. If you don't believe in or understand this connection, you will not act to fix it if it is "broke."

Perhaps we can look at it this way. A girl's father is her first "boyfriend". The relationship with this "boyfriend" sets up the foundation for how she views other males.

A girl's father is her first "boyfriend."

Additionally, girls need to feel love from an adult male. Why a male? Because fathers "love" differently than mothers. Before you have a knee-jerk reaction and label me a sexist, consider the different kinds of love you experience. The type of love you get from your spouse is different from the love you feel from your parents. Love from different genders and relationships fills different needs. We are programmed to strive to have these needs met.

When I was in my early twenties I was well loved by my parents and family. I was also priviledged with a close network of male friends (in public they would be referred to as "the guys" or the "gang") that I built up during my school and army experiences. Though we were guys, I can honestly say that I loved them and that they loved me. (And I still do love them though we are separated by hundreds of miles and rarely visit or speak.

Father-daughter times help ensure sexual purity.

After all, we are guys.) Yet, even though love and acceptance surrounded me from many different people and relationships, I felt a deep longing. I needed love from a woman.

Readers, you know the need I'm talking about. It's the need that keeps you up at night and can eclipse all other needs. And when I found the woman that loved me none of the logistics mattered. It didn't matter that Julia lived seven hundred and thirty two miles away, a drive I could make in ten hours (you do the math). It didn't matter that we were raised within two different cultures, I in Connecticut, she in North Carolina. She filled that aching need (even though I was so loved and accepted from other sources) and I would do anything to be with her.

The need to be loved and accepted within an exclusive relationship is common to human beings. After all ninety eight percent of us get married. Stay with me here. I need for you to understand the importance of Daddy Love to a girl and the relationship that Daddy Love has on the sexual behavior of girls. I'm using first person analogies because I don't want to bog you down with psychobabble and multi syllabic ten-dollar words.

So, can you admit now that there are different kinds of love and that love meets different needs when it comes from different sources? Good. Now I'm going to present another idea to you. The type of love we need changes as our age changes. I would have never left my family and friends for the love of a girl when I was sixteen. I would not have left when I was eighteen. But at twenty-three I could have a local fan club thousands strong and I still would have hit the road.

We need different types of love from different sources at different times of our lives. From roughly eleven to seventeen, girls have an intense need to know that they are loved and approved of (deemed worthy) by their father.

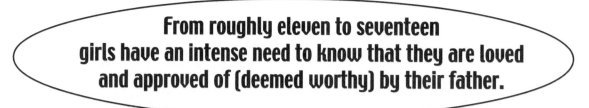

From roughly eleven to seventeen girls have an intense need to know that they are loved and approved of (deemed worthy) by their father.

An eleven to seventeen-year-old girl needs Daddy Love. She won't need this love at this level of intensity forever, but she will need it at this time. She needs it for many reasons. She needs to know that she is "ok" from a man's perspective. She needs to know that she is attractive and acceptable from a male point of view. She needs to know that her "first boyfriend" views her as intelligent and mature. If the "father" in her life does not meet these needs then she will be compelled to have them met elsewhere.

If she can't get these needs met at home she will look for a male outside the home to meet them. And it is this search that makes her vulnerable.

Does she think, "Daddy doesn't pay me enough attention so I'm going to have sex with Billy?" No. The need is subconscious, as is the drive to fill it. Though in extreme cases, a teen-aged girl will consciously have sex with a boy to "get back" at Daddy.

Girls of emotionally distant or absent fathers are at higher risk for early sexual activity. The lack of Daddy Love (or the perception of lack of love because that love has not been communicated) leads the daughter to seek affirmation that she is worthy of love from other men (boys).

The death of a father does not create the same increased risk response. If a father's absence is caused by death it does not create a feeling of unworthiness in the daughter because the daughter has not been rejected. She can process the death and understand why her father is absent from her life.

The women I mentioned earlier were almost always victims of the absence of Daddy Love. Or even worse, victims of Daddy abuse. They would come forward after the workshop and share their stories. "My dad was always negative towards me. He never had anything good to say to me when I was a girl. Boys paid attention to me so I gave them what they wanted. I was pregnant at sixteen." Or, "My dad paid the bills and never beat or hurt us. He just managed me and my sister. He never said I looked good, or was pretty, or that he loved me. I can't remember one time he even touched me, let alone hug me. Boys at my school said and did all those things. I wanted to hear 'I love you' from a guy so much that it seemed 'ok' to give them sex."

I always give them a hug and express my regret. If they have daughters I ask what they are doing to help their daughter in this regard. It always makes me so happy when they motion over their shoulder toward some embarrassed guy. "Oh he's great, he spends so much time with my girl(s)." It is distressing when I find out there is no man nor has there ever been. If you are a single mother, don't be upset at this point. There is a "Daddy Need" solution for you and your family that we will get to shortly.

Mom, in regards to Daddy Love you (I'm writing this chapter to mom because research shows that the majority of parenting book purchasers are women) are in one of four situations.

1. Your husband is meeting his daughter(s) need to feel "Daddy Love."

2. There is a man in the house but he does not maintain an intimate relationship with your daughter or let your daughter know she occupies a "special place" in his heart

3. There is no man in the house and no source of Daddy Love.

4. A surrogate Daddy is filling this role.

Let's take these one at a time. Let's say you have a DDD (Daughter Distant Dad, Pronounced Duh). Mothers often ask me, "How do I know if my husband is meeting this need?" I always answer, "You already know."

Mothers, in your heart of hearts you know if your husband is meeting this "Daddy Love" role with your daughter. Take a moment and ask yourself this question, "Is my husband doing everything he can (or anything at all) to let our daughter know she is loved, valued, appreciated, and approved of by him?" One of the easiest ways to appraise this is to ask another question, "Does my husband ever spend one-on-one time with our daughter?"

If the answer is "no" what do you do? You could go to him and plead passionately that he pay more attention to "His" daughter. You could show him the stats and make him read this chapter. (And cry while doing it) You could tell him that he has let you down and that this is one more way that he has not fulfilled his marital responsibilities while you point out all his other numerous violations and deficiencies. None of the above techniques will work, but you will feel better.

Instead, sit hubby down and explain to him how important he is to his daughter's sexual health. Have him read this chapter. Ideally he should be reading this book with you and discussing each chapter as well as filling out the action points after each chapter. Ideally. If your husband is showing no interest in this book or your concern over your daughter's sexual development then this is the one chapter you must really push. Take the sports section from the paper (or the whole paper) and tell him he will only get it back after he reads this chapter. Or, if you really want to play hardball, hide the remote.

If your husband will not get involved or increase his level of connection with his daughter . . . If he shows no interest in this book or your efforts to protect and guide your daughters sexual well being . . . if he refuses to show interest in, or to even discuss the contents then at least force him to read and sign the following statement. The "Acknowledgement of Impact Contract" is available as a whole page contract in the reproducible section (R.12). If you have to do this I recommend you run it off and present it to him.

Acknowledgement of Impact Contract

Girls who have a distant or no relationship with their father are two and one half times more likely to experience a teen pregnancy. Girls who do not feel loved or 'deemed worthy' by their fathers are two and one half times more likely to engage in risky sexual behavior.

I have read and understand
the above concept _____

Above statement should be signed by biological father as well as stepfather, where applicable. Signed form should be stored in secure location in case risky sexual behavior does occur on the part of teen daughter and father complains about cost of counseling, termination of education, drug use and medical therapy associated with teen pregnancy. Document should also be stored in the case teen conception does take place and father complains about cost associated with delivery, medications, and general support of daughter and baby. This may result in loss of bass boat or other toys.

Ok, let's say he's read the chapter and wants to be more involved with his daughter. He now knows that if he does not want a sexually active or pregnant daughter, he better get more involved in her life. He nods and agrees that he will show more interest and spend more time. You feel better. You hug. Music plays. The emotionally charged meeting is over. Everything will be better. Wrong.

You see, your husband wants to make you happy and may even understand what you want him to do. After you get his importance to your daughter through his thick head (if you get it through) he will nod his head and say he will do better. Nothing will change. Why? I think it has something to do with the fact that some men are stupid.

You see, when women come to men with emotional needs and desires, we want to please you, we just don't know how. We are men. When my wife comes crying and screaming to me that she is overwhelmed with the pressures and duties of being a wife, mother, and business partner, I just don't get it. But if she asks me if I can run the vacuum through the house that day, run errands or bathe the baby, I get it.

Men relate to actions, not feelings.

What does this have to do with getting hubby to show more love and acceptance to his daughter? Everything. He may understand his daughter's need for him. But if you are having this conversation with him he obviously does not know how to meet those needs. He doesn't know what to do. He's not a bad man, just a typical man. What's the solution? Go get his planner, daytimer, palm pilot or calendar. Give him a simple task. Remember that he may not understand emotional need, but he will understand an assignment. And he can meet your daughter's emotional needs by completing a series of assignments, and in the process, build new skills.

A father may not understand his daughter's emotional needs but he will understand an assignment to spend time with her.

Let me explain. Now that you have his planner and his attention you must act quickly. (Keeping in mind the male attention span) Find the next Saturday morning and pencil in, "8:30 - 9:30 Breakfast out w/Susan." He'll do it. Why? Because it's in his planner and he is a man and men do what is in their planner. If he does not use any organizational device then put it on a sticky note and stick it to his mirror. This is just the beginning.

He will do it. See, his mystified male mind will be relieved that you have boiled down this complex emotional need into a simple task. "Duh, take Susan to breakfast, Susan know I love her, Susan not have sex and Wife leave alone." This is the first task you ask him to meet. You don't want to overwhelm the poor guy. If he was comfortable spending time one-on-one with his daughter he would already by doing it. If he fails to meet his breakfast obligation nag him until he bleeds. He is a man so you might have to tie in his needs with his daughter's needs. "You can play golf after you spend some time out with Susan."

Don't be afraid

Ask your daughter if she would like to go out to eat.

This breakfast, or errand, or lunch meeting will take place each week. How do you know? Each week you will put some type of one on one contact with his daughter in his planner. Don't make the mistake of putting something like, "8:30-10:30 time with Susan." He won't do it. You didn't tell him what to do during that time. Put something like, "8:30-10:30 take Susan to mall to pick out new soccer cleats" He'll do it.

Now prepare him for his daughter's reaction to this new overture. It will go something like this, "Honey how about going out to breakfast with me this Saturday?"
    "Oh Dad, I'd rather eat dirt."

You see, teens don't know what they really deeply want. If they did they wouldn't be teens. Somewhere in the very center of whom she is, your daughter will be celebrating the fact that Daddy wants to spend time with her. Somehow this celebration will be occurring at the same time she will be feigning disinterest. Don't allow your husband to be put off. Remember that manual I told you about earlier. The one somehow given out to every teen in America at the onset of puberty. In it there is a commandment that says, "Thou shalt act repulsed at the idea of spending time with your parents."

I once got a call from a father who I was working with on recovering his relationship with his daughter.   The previous week I had given him the Saturday morning breakfast assignment. Because of his schedule he had taken his daughter out for breakfast on a school day. "I did the breakfast thing like you told me to," he started. He didn't sound encouraged.
    "Oh, How did it go?"
    "We fought the whole morning. First she would not make up her mind where she wanted to eat so then when I picked a place she didn't like it. Then she made fun of the clothes I was wearing. She made me sit in the back of the restaurant so none of her friends would see us on their way to school. Then she made fun of the way I eat. I broke some kind of coolness rule. Finally I dropped her off at school and she barely said 'Bye.'"
    I replied, "She had a great time."
    "Oh?"
    "She absolutely loved it. Right now she is telling all her girlfriends at school how her daddy took her out and how he wants to do it once a week."
    "You're kidding?'
    "She is looking forward to the next time you go out. Trust me. While you do this I want you to notice how your relationship changes while you're at home. Not while you're on your 'dates' but while you're at home."

After several months that father reported what most fathers report when I send them on this "dating" exercise. Things were getting better at home throughout the week. Less partying, less rebellion, less promiscuous behavior.

There is more good news in all of this. A Father could do a lousy job at reaching out to his daughter and the effect will still be positive. He could be a hopeless case at building an intimate relationship with his daughter but the effort will still bring some rewards in changed behavior. In other words, any attempt by the father to create a closer relationship with the daughter yields a positive adjustment for risk behaviors.

As with each chapter in this book, a book could be written on this concept. But you don't have time for twelve different books. However, if you are open to additional reading you will find books that correlate with each chapter listed in the back. There are some great books written by men for men on this topic. They are listed in the resource section.

We could go on to further specific instruction for our Daughter Disengaged Dad. We could cover how to praise how to communicate, etc. But none of this will matter if he does not spend one-on-one time with his daughter. Is it this simple? Can a man send the vital messages of love and worthiness to his daughter by continuously spending one-on-one time with her? Yes, if Dad changes. You see this is more about Dad than Daughter.

**You see this is more about Dad than Daughter.
Even if Dad has the nurturing gifts of a brick, his relationship
skills will improve simply by spending the time one-on-one.**

These meetings will matter if your husband changes. Now here's the great part: these one-on-one times (if they happen on a regular predictable basis) *will* change the way your husband deals with your daughter. Even men have the ability to learn. Let's go for another of my goofy analogies. Let's say I gave you a rowboat and oars and told you to row around a course marked on a lake. Imagine you don't know how to row and you have a deep fear of the water. I don't tell you how to row or even where to sit. I don't lecture you or even place the oars in the oar-locks. (Just as you won't lecture Dad on how to grow more intimate with his daughter, you know he dislikes being lectured and he won't do it if you lecture him.) I don't even help you put the boat in the water. Once a week I make you go rowing. I don't get in the boat with you and I don't communicate with you before, during, or after the session.

You would drag the boat from the stern down to the water, get or fall in, and start going around in circles. You would eventually discover where to sit. Out of the three choices most rowboats offer you will most likely get this right the first time. Your innate ability to learn and reason on the fly will show you. Eventually you will discover the primary absurdity of rowboats: the fact that you face backward in order to go forward.

Sooner or later, probably part of the way through the first or second session, you will get the thing around the course once. It will be ugly but you will do it. All without one bit of instruction. After several sessions you will start to pick up the subtleties of your new activity. You have wanted to quit several times because of how sore your arms get, they hurt. (Just as your husband will get hurt in this new territory.) You've known where to sit for several sessions but one day while you are splashing around (hating me for giving you this stupid assignment, as your husband will hate you) you make a discovery. You realize that if you pull more with your back than with your arms your arms don't hurt as much the following week. You make another big breakthrough when you realize that you can keep the boat going in a straight line by pointing the boat where you want to go then looking directly astern. You spot an object on shore and stay lined up. No more looking over your shoulder all day. (That hurt)

I show up a few months later and you blaze around the course with a triumphant smile on your face.

Did I ever instruct or go with you? No. All I did was make sure each session happened. I called your house, harassed you at work, and cancelled all your magazine subscriptions. I didn't teach you anything about rowing. You wouldn't have listened, anyway. I just made sure you spent the time. You now compete in rowing.

All I did was make sure each session happened.

Could you learn how to do something that you were afraid of, had no experience in, and didn't even want to do? Yes. Could you learn it with no instruction, only contact time? Absolutely. Can your husband learn how to build a close and approving relationship with his daughter? Yes.

Your husband can learn to create a nurturing relationship with his daughter. Even if he's afraid, reluctant and clueless, he has the built in ability to adapt to the emotional situations that unfold. You don't have to sign him up for a touchy-feely course, coach him or worry him.

You just make sure he spends one on one time with his daughter.
He can use his natural ability to learn and adapt to develop the
empathetic and communicative skills he will need.

He will get sore and want to quit. He will get hurt and try to back off. He won't tell you he's going to stop with "this one on one thing." No, instead he will employ the "slow fade" that men are so good at. Don't let him. Take his golf clubs. Manipulate, cajole, praise profusely, do whatever you have to do. Just make sure his "rowing sessions" happen.

When you get him to once a week, up it to twice and then three times ...We don't want him to get comfortable. Eventually the one on one time he spends with his daughter won't be as staged or forced. It will become something "they do."

So, you are going to have him spend one on one time and you are going to have him touch. Touch is important. Teach him to hug his daughter and say, "I love you." Teach him how to do it casually and easily. The two of you may have to practice. Maybe a hug is too much to ask for at first. Perhaps you should start him off with a pat and positive comment. Role-play.

Father Daughter touch is important.

You sit where your daughter usually eats breakfast. Have your husband walk in, give you a brief rub on the shoulder and say, "Luv ya." Walk him through it several times. Then have him execute the real thing on his daughter the next morning. Incorporate this touching/positive message program into your one-on-one father-daughter outing program. He can do it. Put it in his planner "Tuesday 7:30 - hug daughter when get home, tell pretty." He'll do it.

Why some men don't touch their daughters affectionately has been studied, analyzed and puzzled over. We're not going to go into it here. Suffice it to say, just like "rowing," even the most emotionally illiterate male can acquire this "skill." So now we have taken a Daughter Disengaged Dad and engaged him. What if there is no Dad?

What if there is no Dad? Get one.

Get one. Although research has shown that the biological father has the greatest effect (either negative or positive), a stepfather, grandfather or other family member can fill this role. This role can *not* be filled by a live-in boyfriend. Any man who has a temporary informal relationship with your family and extended family cannot fill this role. Do not "hire" anyone to be surrogate dad whom you yourself do not trust and love.

This role cannot be filled by a live in boyfriend.

Does your little girl's grandfather live near by? Would he be interested in being, "Daddy?" Pitch it to him. Could he pick your daughter up from school and spend some time with her once or twice a week? Perhaps you do have an extended family member who already is spending time with your daughter. Could you meet with him and go over this chapter? Give him "permission" to praise and guide, to build a more supportive relationship. Danger: a live in or any other type of boyfriend absolutely cannot fill this role. If you do try to find a surrogate Dad for your daughter make sure this man has a permanent status in your life and your extended family's life. If he starts to build this relationship and then departs, he becomes one more "rejecting father."

What if there is a Father but he does not live in the home?

If the biological father does not live in the home all the above still applies. A divorced father can still make a difference on this front. He can make a difference, but it will obviously take more effort on his part. He can still spend one-on-one time, he can still build a close relationship and he can still meet his daughter's need to be loved by a father figure.

Studies have shown that close relationships can be created with non-resident parents. One survey found that, "children are protected from risk behaviors when experiencing the highest degree of closeness, caring and satisfaction with parental relationship, whether resident or non-resident mother or father."[5]   Another study isolated visitation with fathers exclusively. The researchers found that, "teens living with a single mother who regularly spend time with their absent father are at lower risk of substance abuse than teens who do not see their father.[6] Though this study measured drug use I believe that it is fair to assume that the positive effect of steady father visitation would carry over to sexual behavior.

Sit down with your ex at a local restaurant and have him sign the "Acknowledgment of Impact Contract" (R.12). Then grab his planner. If you are fighting with your ex, now is the time to isolate that conflict from your daughter. She doesn't have to know you hate each other. She just wants to feel Daddy Love. Dad can be more involved than once every two-week visitation. He can pick her up from practice, shuttle her to commitments, and run her to the dentist.

What if you are on your own? What if you can't come up with a surrogate father and the biological father is several states away? What if he is uninvolved and has made it clear he wants to stay that way?

What do all the experts have to offer the embattled unsupported single mother? Surprisingly, some good news. Highly involved single moms can "out perform" uninvolved or average parents with intact marriages. One study looked at hands-on parenting and its effect on teen health. The study defined "hands on" parents as parents who establish a household culture where they consistently set down rules and expectations for their teens' behavior and monitor what their teen does. The study goes on to define hands-on parents as parents who monitor TV and Internet viewing and music. They also set curfews and stay on top of their child's activities before and after school and on weekends. (Sound familiar?)

The study found that, "Being a 'hands-on' parent can significantly lower the teen's risk regardless of family structure. A teen living with a single mother who is 'hands on,' is at lower risk of substance abuse than the average teen living in a two-parent household.7

So, Unsupported Single Moms, you may not be able to provide Daddy Love but you can make up for it in other ways. You can produce a child that values abstinence not by buying, treating and spoiling but by standing firm and setting guidelines and expectations. You can not be "Dad" but you can implement all the other strategies in this book. You can monitor, set curfews, guide purchasing decisions, and protect your child from Sex Saturated-Media. You can be involved and "hands-on." You can be what I call a Super Single Mom. (SSM pronounced sim)

The most important thing a father can do for his children is to love their mother.
–Theodore Hesburgh

Action Plan

As a result of this chapter what are you going to do and when are you going to do it?

Examples - *I will take Susan out once a week starting May 23rd. I will try to touch her affectionately and tell her I love her everyday.*

I will sit down with George and go over this chapter with him on Friday night.

I will praise and support my husband as he tries to build a closer relationship with Jill.

_____

_____

_____

_____

_____

_____

_____

_____

_____

_____

_____

The place of the father in the modern suburban
family is a very small one, particularly
if he plays golf.
– Bertrand Russell

You are the bows from which your children
as living arrows are sent forth.
– Kahlil Gibran

CHAPTER 14

Your Marriage, Your Home Environment and Your Teen's Sexual Behavior

I stated in chapter three that we were going to move from easier to more difficult strategies. Having a good marriage must be hard or so many people would not be getting un-married. Monitoring your teen's social life and media exposure may be difficult. But this is one of the last chapters because having a healthy marriage will surely take even more effort.

You're thinking, "Keith, I bought this book because I wanted to protect my child from pre-marital sex. If I had wanted a marriage book I would have bought one. I already have a ton of relationship books." Good, you may need them.

What does the state of your marriage have to do with whether your fourteen-year-old has intercourse or not?
Everything.

What does the environment in your home have to do with teen sexuality?
Everything.

Your marriage is your teen's first blueprint for the role of sex in his/her life. Kind of scary. You think your child does not listen. He listens to everything you say. You may not like the result, but he does listen. And he studies. He watches, and takes notes. Your teen studies everything you do within the family and within your marriage relationship. Your teen knows whether you and your husband have a physical relationship or not.

Your Teen studies the relationship you have with your spouse.

You may tell your teen to, "save sex until marriage." You may tell your teen that, "The best plan is for you to wait and then enjoy a wonderful physical relationship within marriage." He hears you but more importantly, he is watching both of you. If he is observing a dysfunctional relationship, then it invalidates everything you have to say about sex, love and marriage.

If your teen is submitted to an unstable marriage then everything you say about sex and love is greeted with skepticism.

If that's what marriage looks like, why wait!

Your teen will listen to what you say about sex and love but more importantly he will measure it against what you are doing about sex and love. If the actions within your marriage are inconsistent with what you are saying then he will dismiss your message as irrelevant.

If you are a single parent, you do not have to worry about displaying an unhealthy picture of marital relations. Your teen does not have a marriage to observe. However, he is still watching you. If your boyfriend sleeps over and stays in your bedroom then your lecture on chastity will be heard but ignored. You will have invalidated it by your actions

A teenager has no opportunity to observe sexual relations between a married man and women first hand. He cannot go to a museum and observe the "healthy marriage exhibit." Likewise, he can't ask to tag along with his science teacher to take notes on "healthy marital communication." He certainly is not going to get a healthy picture of sexual marital relations from the media. (Think, *Married with Children*).

If one of the greatest risk factors for teens is growing up in a single parent home then it seems like we should be doing everything possible to keep homes two parent.

Working on your relationship with your spouse will help you avoid one of the largest health risks to your children: a single parent home.

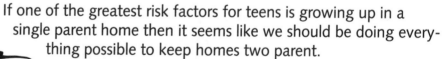

I was once working with a family who had a son in crisis. The teen was using drugs, was sexually active and in danger of flunking out. I get this call a lot. Both biological parents were in the home and they were the perfect picture of American family success. They lived in a large home that overlooked a golf course. Dad earned a high six figure salary with a Fortune Five Hundred company, while mom volunteered in the schools and busied herself with civic causes. I'm not sure if I've ever worked in a sicker household. Dad managed his family like I imagined he

How could I have anything to do with my child's sexual behavior?

managed his professional life. He was impersonal and very interested in efficiency when dealing with his family. He would spend time with his family in chunks that he would block off on his calendar months in advance. He felt if he spent two weeks with his wife and children at an exotic location then he was meeting his requirements (and doing it efficiently, I observed). The fact that he was unavailable to them during their daily lives did not alarm him. He fired off orders and actually wrote memos to stand in his absence. He could not understand why they weren't followed like the ones at work. Mom was in denial about Dads lack of commitment to her and the children. Both were very concerned with the way the family was viewed by the community.

One morning, after struggling to get on his calendar, I met Dad at a restaurant. I've learned you don't tell a man what to do while sitting in that man's office or home. After small talk I got right to the point, "I want you and your wife to go on a three-day retreat." After a moment of silence he replied, "I hired you to straighten my kid out, not poke around in my marriage."

"Oh," I muttered, "You want me to focus exclusively on Jeff's needs?"

"Yes, I'm authorizing you to do whatever you have to do to get him back on track and I'm willing to back you up on whatever limitations we should put in place."

"That's great. Would you and your wife go on a three day retreat in order to help your son?" Silence. "I'm going to ask you and your wife to change your behavior and the way you communicate with your son. You do not communicate well with each other. You disagree on curfews, fight in front of him, and undermine each other's authority. In short, I'm not sure if your marriage has what it takes to create the environment Jeff needs to get better."

"I don't see how my relationship with my wife causes my son to make bad decisions about girls and cause his grades to decline. (Dad never would acknowledge the drug use.)

"I know you don't see the connection, that's why I'm here."

"Well, I may be able to spend some time with her."

"That doesn't sound like a commitment." I then went into a ten-minute dissertation on the importance of a healthy marriage to the products of that marriage. I further explained that it is not enough that the marriage not be in distress, but that it is important that the child know it is not in distress. His response was to question my credibility and education level. I pointed out that he had hired me knowing I only possessed a four-year degree in elementary education. He had checked out my references with other families and had made a warm appraisal of my abilities when he hired me. After defending my background, I asked, "Will you work on your marriage in measurable ways so that I can know that you are working on your marriage?

"I'm not sure I'm willing to report to you on counseling and retreat sessions."

"I'm not asking for a report on what happens at sessions. I just want to know they are happening." Silence. Stony stare that I'm sure can chill a board meeting. I continued, "If you are not willing to invest time in your relationship with your wife, then I can no longer work with Jeff. You

see I value my time as well as you value yours, and I know all the effort I put into Jeff will be futile if the environment in your home does not change." I call this the "I'll quit ultimatum" It may seem harsh but it usually works.

They went on that three-day retreat and got counseling. Dad started spending more time at home. I was never able to get him to spend one-on-one time with his son but he would spend time as a threesome. Jeff's behavior improved as his parents' behavior improved. They had gained credibility in his eyes. It is hard for parents to tell their children not to deviate from healthy practices when all the child sees is two people in a combative unhealthy relationship. Once the marriage was perceived to be legitimate, the edicts emerging from that marriage held more legitimacy.

I'm not comfortable!

Jeff began to respect curfews and respond to his parents in a more positive way. He agreed with me to stop having intercourse even though I could not get him to give up sex. His parents and I hadn't stopped his drug use but he was now accepting the consequences if we caught him. Things were moving along. Then I got fired. Dad called me from his office and let me know my services would no longer be needed. When I pointed out that there was still work to do he replied, "With the excellent guidance you have given us I believe we can take it from here." I was going to ask if he had discussed the decision to "take it from here" with his wife but I already knew the answer.

I received a note from his wife about six months later. Apparently she was not allowed to call. It seems Dad had found his new role uncomfortable so he pulled what I called a "slow fade" until he was back to being his self-absorbed self.

Think about it. The health of his family had shown improvement because his marriage had improved and it was still not enough reward for him to continue raising his level of involvement. His marriage had changed. He got uncomfortable. He slid back. I believe he knew I would observe "the slide" back to marital dysfunction so he let me go. The note revealed that they had stopped working with their therapist about six months ago. (I had recommended a marital therapist in town). The note ended thanking me for my efforts and then requesting that I, "Please not respond by phone or mail."

I tell you this story to illustrate a point. Even though the child's behavior improved and the home environment was getting better, Dad felt the need to stop what was happening. He believed he could go back to his former behavior and the positive changes that took place would survive. This type of denial is rampant among American parents. Despite all the evidence that their efforts were helping Jeff, the parents did not want to continue working on their marriage. They wanted the problem with their son to be both "outside" them and "outside" their marriage. Parents have a difficult time accepting that the health of their marriage has a strong influence on the behavior of their children. It is also strenuous for them to accept that the environment in their home affects teen behavior.

Parents have difficulty accepting the influence of their union on their child's general behavior. It is even more difficult for them to accept the influence their marriage and general home environment has on their child's sexual behavior. My experience and the experiences of others have revealed this disconnect. Even when faced with the improving condition of their son, the above family would not continue the effort. While parents shuttle their teens from specialist to specialist, while they seek prescriptions for anti-depressants and hyperactivity medication, while they drive their daughters to Crisis Pregnancy Centers, while they attend numerous teacher conferences, the answer to whatever ails the child may lie in their own marriage relationship. While parents pursue the cure, diagnoses, magic technique, birth control, right school environment, or right therapist for their children, the statistics march on:

A teenager very much left to her own devices, learning by trial and error, easily influenced by peers, and relying heavily on them for essential emotional support and lacking critical input, guidance and direction from adults, is unlikely to observe two loving, caring, parents who function as role models for successful interaction in marriage.[1]

Analyzing the statistical body of evidence a powerful consensus has emerged that, "From a child's point of view, according to a growing body of social research, the most supportive household is one with two biological parents in a low-conflict marriage."[2] (Underline mine)

There is a tremendous amount of research showing that parental inconsistency leads to children being more aggressive, more defiant and more oppositional.[3] (Underline mine)

Recent research suggests that closeness with parents serves as a protective factor against emotional distress, substance use, early sexual activity, and suicide thoughts or attempts.[4] (Underline mine)

On summary of a large body of studies done by different groups with diverse backgrounds and agendas, "Time and time again, the home environment emerges as central in shaping health outcomes for American youth.[5]

I believe that it is difficult for parents to accept the role their union plays in their child's well being because it would require looking at themselves rather than the child. We do not like to believe we are part or cause of any problem. It is much easier to blame any teen-risk behavior, sexual or otherwise, on the teen. I believe it may have something to do with pride. I know this first hand.

My marriage to Julia was in crises when we walked out the church doors. I will not go into the details here but suffice it to say that our first years together were not ideal. I kept on trying to change her so things would get better. I refused to see how my actions and negative personality traits (I would not acknowledge that I had negative personality traits) could possibly be causing the disharmony in our marriage. I believed the fault lay with her, or our financial situation, or her family or how busy we were. I knew it could not be me. How Julia stayed with me those years I do not know. I want to believe it was the first few but I know it took me longer than that to realize the man in the mirror was the problem.

One of the hardest things I have ever done is admit to myself that I had "some serious problems" that I needed to work on. I needed to change. Since the time I started working on me and admitted my role in sabotaging my marriage things have gotten better. I still slip but I don't slide as far.

Just as I had to look at my role in our marriage you have to look at the role of your marriage in your family. Study after study links a negative family environment to early sexual activity in young people. Well, if a positive family environment is so pivotal to adolescent sexual well being, what is pivotal to having a positive and healthy family environment? Answer; having a positive and healthy marriage. Or, to quote a license plate, "If Mama ain't happy ain't nobody happy." From a child's perspective that bumper and sticker would read, "If Mama and Daddy ain't happy with each other then ain't nobody happy."

If Mama and Daddy ain't happy with each other then ain't nobody happy.

The purpose of the chapter is not to give you all the answers you need to improve your marriage. The purpose of this chapter is to get you to recognize that the health of your marriage influences your child's sexual behavior. Do you have to have a perfect relationship? No, there is no such thing. Dear reader you know as you read this whether your marriage is affecting your family in a positive or negative way.

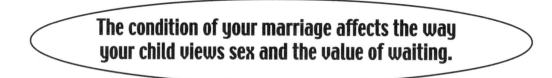

The condition of your marriage affects the way your child views sex and the value of waiting.

For a minute be your child in your house watching you and your spouse. You're sitting at the breakfast table, what do you see? You're riding in the back of the mini van while you and your spouse sit up front, what do you hear? You're lying in bed just before falling asleep while you and your spouse move about the house what do you hear and how do you feel? Do you feel loved?

Are you secure that Mommy and Daddy are going to stay together? Or can you hardly wait to get out of the house to be with your friends?

We are reluctant to work on our marriages because we instinctively know that it will involve personal change . . . and that admits that there is something to change. And admitting that there is something to change is synonymous with admitting that we may be doing something wrong. . . and Pride hates to admit that we may be at fault. I know.

The good news is that marital change can happen. Unlike the family previously described, I have seen it happen and stick. If your marriage is shaky or combative then it probably has been for a long time. You have not put the energy into changing it. The difference is that now you are viewing the health of your marriage in relation to the health of your children. For some reason we are reluctant to work on a marriage that is "broke" for the sake of the marriage alone. I have, however, seen and read of positive marital change taking place because of stressors outside the marriage . . . to save a business, to reach a goal, because of an illness, or to save the health of a child.

Perhaps you and your spouse may have settled for an "average, combative, suburban, luke warm marriage" because anything else would take too much effort. But that was back when you were thinking of yourselves as the only people affected by the level of interaction in your union. Now whether or not your child has intercourse in the sixth grade has been tied to the health of your marriage. If your child experiments with drugs or is violent has been tied to the health of your marriage. Kind of changes things doesn't it? So if you haven't pulled yourselves together for yourselves then do it for your children.

Of course, if everything is fine then carry on.

We are going to talk about two marriages now. The one you have and the one your child perceives you have. You can change the one your child perceives you have tomorrow. Changing the one you actually have will take longer. I'm going to tell you three things you can start doing tomorrow to change the marriage your child thinks you have.

1. Stop Fighting

Stop fighting in front of your child. Stop shouting, arguing, threatening to leave and demeaning each other in front of your teen. It is very difficult for your teen to save sex for marriage when the marriage they are seeing is at war. Would you wait to be married to you? Notice I'm not asking you to stop fighting; you won't be able to do that overnight. Just stop shouting and arguing in any situation where your teen can hear or see you. Don't expose your teen to a loveless house or they will look for "love" elsewhere.

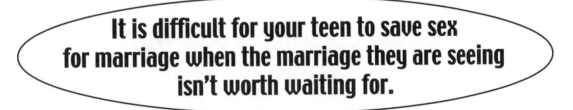

It is difficult for your teen to save sex for marriage when the marriage they are seeing isn't worth waiting for.

2. Start Meeting

While working with families I noticed one constant in families that were in crises. The parents never talked. I don't mean they refused to communicate with each other, I mean they never *talked.* As we have discussed earlier, families live at an incredible pace. And at the helm of this ship rushing from one activity to another you will often find two overworked and disconnected parents. Of course they talk. But it's mostly an exchange of facts based on the urgency of the next task. *Who is picking up Billy from practice? Did you see Jason's grades? Did you pay the credit card bill? Please drop by the store and get some laundry detergent on the way home, oh, what time will you be home?* So much communication goes into the urgency of the moment that there isn't time for any planning or in-depth discussion.

Think of meeting together each night as a pre-emptive strike against future conflict!

While counseling, positioned between a husband and wife rehashing the day's fight or emergency, I have often discovered that the crises could have been avoided with a little communication the night before. Try to put aside ten minutes for each other just before you go to bed. Then you may get a brief moment to discuss your dreams, visions, and feelings rather than the hurried logistics of running a family. After you spend a little time speaking, as adults that have a relationship outside of being parents, go over the schedule for the next day. I know, the reason you set aside this time was so that you could get out of parenting mode. But, if you spend just a little time planning the next day, Billy won't get left at soccer practice and Dad will actually be at his daughter's recital rather than wondering where everyone is when he gets home. If you meet together each night, you may avoid some of the little misunderstandings that can lead to fighting in front of your children.

3. Eat Dinner Together

Make a strong effort to eat at least one meal a day as a family. Pretty deep, huh? Eating together as a family says, "We are a family and you matter." There is more happening when you eat together than just consuming food in a group. Eating together is of more importance than we have time to go into here. If you have not been eating together as a family and there is disharmony in the home then you and your kids may not enjoy the first few meals. But even as your teenager is giving you grief because you called him away from the TV to sit down for a meal, he is celebrating inside. Part of him is saying, "Mommy and Daddy must love me because they are taking time out and going through the effort of getting us all together. Everything must be 'ok' between them because they are working together to serve this meal."

Eating together is powerful

You picked up this book because you wanted to keep your teen safe from premarital sex... and I'm telling you to eat together as a family? Eating together shows the headship the marital union has over the family. Eating together as a family models the execution of traditional marital function. Eating together is a powerful way of communicating marital well being to your children. And now to address the reason you picked up this book; eating together is a powerful promoter of sexual abstinence.

In the youngest age group, 12-14 year olds, teens who eat dinner regularly with a parent are about half as likely to have had sex as other teens their age, and those who are close to a parent are less than half as likely to have had sex.[6]

There is a strong positive correlation between eating dinner with a parent, being close to a parent and sexual abstinence.[7]

Super Single Parents please note that the research shows that eating together is still a powerful family activity for you. You cannot model your marriage while you eat. But you are still sending the message that family is important. You will still be making a statement that will resonate with your children. You will still be forced to communicate with them and they will be forced to communicate with you. Sharing a meal together as a family conveys love and security to your children whether you are married or not.

Don't sleep past your hour of opportunity and miss the gift of children

I'm not talking about munching down on some instant meal in front of *MTV*. I'm talking about sitting down in chairs around a table where the food is served from a common source and at least part of the meal took preparation. Do it. Even if you don't know how to work the stove and have no time it can be done. Whenever you cook something double or triple the serving. That way you save time because you can eat off it over several days. Just work in *your* food slowly. We don't want to kill them while we save them.

I know I can't solve your marital problems but *you* can. I do know that the three activities I mention will produce an immediate change in the environment of your home. Stop fighting in front of your family and start meeting together and watch your children change. Actually sit down and eat with them and you will feel the atmosphere in the home change for the better. (Even though these meals may seem to you like one more opportunity to argue with your teen they will be doing some good.) After you put these emergency measures in place your children will perceive a different parent team. That will be the change in the marriage they think you have made. Only you know that you have just scratched the surface. They can be living under a different marriage within two days. If your union is "bad broke," it will take more effort than Keith's "pot hole patch" three-step program. However, I can assure you that the three things I'm asking you to do will have a dramatic and immediate impact on your family. To change the marriage you will need to go deeper. We can't do it here. You will have to pursue this with other tools, methods, and people. Several resources are listed in back.

Investing time in your marriage is a very effective strategy for encouraging abstinence in your teen.

They are watching you. They are hearing you. They will value what you value. You are their example of the proper role of sex; abstinence until marriage and a fulfilling sex life afterward. Give them a positive example to follow.

Action Plan

As a result of this chapter what are you going to do and when are you going to do it?

Examples - *I will meet with my spouse on _____/_____/_____ and tell her that this time I am honestly interested in improving our relationship.*

We will schedule a three-day romantic get away and take it by _____/_____/_____

_____

_____

_____

_____

_____

_____

_____

_____

_____

_____

_____

_____

_____

_____

It is not only what we do that we are held responsible, but also for what we do not do.
– Moliere

Marriage is great and sex within marriage is great!

Even as the cell is the unit of the organic body, so the family is the unit of society.

– Ruth Nanda Anshen

Dear Reader,

I have enjoyed spending time with you. I hope you find the information in this book helpful. I would like to take the time to apologize if I appeared arrogant or crass. Saying difficult things in a manner acceptable to all takes eloquence. And writing eloquently takes more words than writing frankly. And frankly, I felt you would more likely use this book if I limited its length and got right to the point.

This is the first printing of *FIGHTING BACK*. I am interested in any ideas you may have for the next edition. If you have advice or a key element you feel I have missed I would like to hear from you. I would also like to hear from you if you felt this book was helpful and what particular area you found most applicable. Also, if you feel that I was wrong in anything contained please contact me with your concerns. Please e-mail your ideas and thoughts to delta@vnet.net. If I use your idea in the next edition I will list your name under "Contributors." I may not be able to respond to all your e-mails but I will try. Please consider sending me anything that would fit in the resource section.

Children First,

Keith J. Deltano
Freedom Farm
Julian, NC
January 3rd 2005

PART THREE

Appendix
(Useful Stuff)

The world is a dangerous place, not because those who do evil, but because of those who look on and do nothing.
– Albert Einstien

Remember, people will judge you by your actions, not your intentions. Your may have a heart of gold – but so does a hard–boiled egg.
– Anon

APPENDIX A

Bibliography/Notes

Chapter 1

1. Lydia A. Shrier, Sion Kim Harris, and William R. Beardslee, "Temporal Associations Between Depressive Symptoms and Self-reported STDs Among Adolescents." Archives of Pediatrics and Adolescent Medicine 156 (2002): 599-606.

2. US News and World Report, May 27, 2002, pp. 40-49

3. National Center for HIV, STD, TB Prevention, Centers for Disease Control, U.S. Department of Health and Human Services. "Tracking the Hidden Epidemics." Database online. www.cdc/gov.com

4. Child's Trend Research Center, Teenage Motherhood Rate Plummets, Chris Michaud, New York Post, December 1, 2003

5. Birthrate Figures For The Nation, Teens, hit Record Lows, NCHS, and CDC, Cheryl Wetzein, The Washington Times, June 25, 2003

6. D.T. Fleming et al., "Herpes Simplex Virus Type 2 in the United States, 1976 to 1994." New England Journal of Medicine 337 (1997:1105-1160

Chapter 2

1. Connect with Kids - The Teen Years "Reforming Youth Issues for Public Consideration and Support" Communications and Community, UCLA, 2000

2. Parents - primary sex educators Concerned women for America Family Planning Perspectives. July 1996.

3. White House Conference on Teenagers: Raising Responsible and Resourceful Youth May 2, 2000

4. White, Sharon A. and Tom Luster. (1992) "Adolescent Sexual Behavior," Adolescence, 27:105 183-191

5. Associated Press Report, Survey of Youth attitudes, Kansas City Star.

Chapter 4

1. Howe, Neil. And Strauss Bill. Children's Defense fund and *13th Generation* Survey of statistics from organization and book

Chapter 7

1. George Comstrock, "The Medium and the Society: The Role of Television in American Life," *Children and Television* (Newbury Park: Sage Publications, 1993

2,3 US News and World Report Compiled in Why Are Kids So Angry. Chris Slane

4. *The Long Hard Road Out Of Hell* by Marilyn Manson. Regan Books 1998

5. Kaiser Family Foundation Media Images and Outcomes 1999

6. White, Joe. <u>That Kids Wish Parents Knew about Parenting.</u> Louisiana: Howard Publishing. 1998

7. McDowell, Josh. Hostetler, Bob. <u>Right From Wrong: What You Need To Know To Help Youth Make Right Choices.</u> Word Publishing. 1994

Chapter 8

1. Paul Pringle, "Vice Squad Legend Now Hunts Cyberporn," Copley News Service, San Diago Union-Tribune, May 19, 1996, p. A-3

2. AltaVista search by Zachary Britton, author of <u>Safty Net:</u> Guiding & Guarding Your Children on the Internet, November 13, 1996, http://www.altavista.digital.com. Oregon. Harvest House. 1998

Chapter 10

1. National Survey of American Attitudes on Substance Abuse VI: Teens National Center on Addiction and Substance Abuse at Columbia University CASA Feb 2001

Chapter 11

1. Jaccard et al 1996, Small and Luster 1994, Building Healthy Futures, The Medical Institute for Sexual Health, 2000 p22

2. Building Healthy Futures, The Medical Institute for Sexual Health, 2000 p.23

Chapter 12

1. "Ignoring an Epidemic" Austin, Tex.: The Medical Institute for Sexual Health, *Media Advisories.* www.medinstitute.org/media/editorial-1.htm.

2. National Center for HIV, STD, TB Prevention, Centers for Disease Control, U.S. Department of Health and Human Services. "Tracking the Hidden Epidemics." Database online. www.cdc/gov.com

3. D.T. Fleming et al., "Herpes Simplex Virus Type 2 in the United States, 1976 to 1994." New England Journal of Medicine 337 (1997: 1105-1160

4. ibid

5. Lisa Remez, "Oral Sex 'Doesn't Count' As More Engage." LifeDate, Family Life Issues. Internet online: www.lutheransforlife.org/lifedate/2001/spring/teens_say_oral_sex_Doesn't_count.html

6. Oral Sex and STDs, Fact Sheet, Centers for Disease Control, Dec. 2000

7. See number 5

8. National Institute of Allergy and Infectious Diseases, National Institutes of Health, Department of Health and Human Services. *Workshop Summary: Scientific Evedence On Condom Effectiveness for Sexually Transmitted Disease Prevention, July 20, 2001*

9. Saifuddin Ahmed et al., "HEV Incidence and Sexually Transmitted Disease Prevelaence Associated with Condom Use: A Population Study in Rakai, Uganda." AIDS 15 (2001 2171-2179

10. *Federal Panel on Condoms Offers Crucial Warnings to Sexually Actine Americans, Says The Medical Institute for Sexual Health..*"NIH Condom Report Press Release. Media Advisories, Austin, Tex.: The Medical Institute for Sexual Health, July 19, 2001

11. A. Wald, A. G. M. Langenberg, K. Link, et al, "Effect of Condoms on Reducing the Transmission of Herpes Simplex Virus Type 2 from Men to Women." *Journal of the American Medical Association* 285 (2001): 3100-3106

12. Sexuality Information and Education Council of the United States (SIECUS) "Non-Coital Behaviors That Put Teens at Risk for HIV and Other STDs." *SHOP Talk: School Health Opportunities and Progress Bulletin 5, no. 22 (2001).*

13. See number 6

14. See number 5

Chapter 13

1. Centers for Disease Control and Prevention. National Study of Adolescent Sexual Behavior. 2000. Atlanta

2,6 Why Are Kids So Angry? H. Chris Slane III, M.A. - Director of Research 1999 - Family First. Tampa, Florida. (p.10-11)

2. Bruce J. Ellis, et. Al. "Quality of Early Family Relationships and Individual Differences in the Timing of Pubertal Maturation in Girls: A Longitudinal Test of an Evolutionary Model" *Journal of Personality and Social Psychology 77,* (August 1999) 387-401. *Child Development, TK*

4,5 Connections That Make a Difference in The Lives of Youth. Dr. R.W. Blum and PM Rinehart. Division of General Pediatrics and Adolescent Health. University of Minnesota.

7 National Survey of American Attitudes on Substance Abuse VI: Teens National Center on Addiction and Substance Abuse at Columbia University (CSA) Feb. 2001

Chapter 14

1. Northam. apbnew.com "Study Finds Bad-Girl Cycle" May 8, 2000

2. Blain Harden, "2-Parent Families Rise After Change In Welfare Laws," New York Times, August 12, 2001

3. Laura Shapiro, "The Myth of Quality Time," *Newsweek,* May 12, 1997, 64 (p.13)

4. Resnick, M.D., et al. 1997 "Protecting Adolescents from Harm: Findings from the National Longitudinal Study on Adolescent Health." Journal of the American Medical Association

5. Reducing the Risk: Connections That Make a Difference in The Lives of Youth. Dr. R.W. Blum and P.M Rinehart.

6,7 The White House Conference on Teenagers: Raising Responsible and Resourceful Youth: Teens and Their Parents in the 21st Century: An Examination of Trends in Teen Behavior And the Role of Parental Involvement" May 2, 2000.

APPENDIX B

Useful Reproducibles

You can learn things from children, how much patience your have, for instance.
– Franklin P. Jones

What I say and do has great effect on my children's developing value system

I'm
the parent

R.2

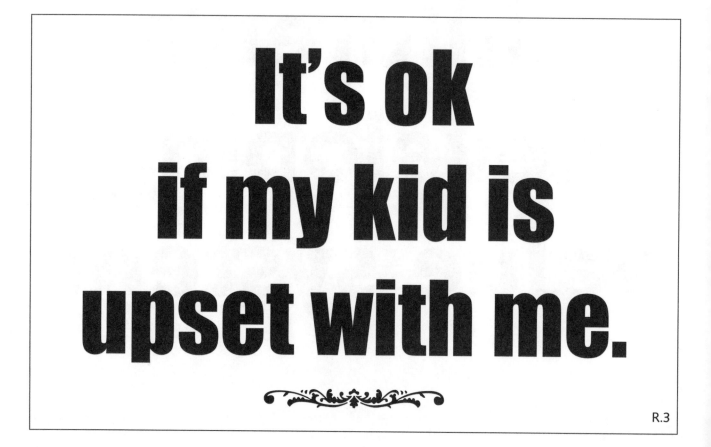

It's ok
if my kid is
upset with me.

R.3

Instructions for the "Tribe Tracker"

When you start filling out the form you may have the following conversation (or something like it):

"Mom, why do you want all this?"

"Because I love you."

"I know that, but you haven't asked for this stuff before"

"I should have, so I'm asking for it now."

"I don't want to give you this info, it's none of your business and you're being intrusive."

"I have every right to know who you're with and what you are doing when you are outside this home. You *earn* the right to be free of my monitoring. Freedom is earned, and it is not granted with age. I want this stuff because I love you"

Have you ever noticed that teenagers take the time to learn all the big words when it comes time to attack you and put you on the defensive? I have worked with teenagers that possessed monosyllabic vocabularies except when arguing with their parents about expectations. Then they would accuse them of being "intrusive," "invasive," "totalitarian" and "constricting."

Try to get every column filled out. Try to get names and numbers for every face that has graced your foyer. You also want the names and numbers for all the voices on the phone. You want every member of the tribe whether you have seen them of not. Pay particular attention to the inner circle. Try to get as much information on the living situations of the inner circle. Are their parents divorced? This is important for many reasons. For example, your child may say she's over Joey's house. If Joey has two houses and you only know about one you have messed up. You need to start to use this list to build a relationship with the parents of the tribe. Some of them probably want to get to know you but they are afraid to call because they don't want to appear "old fashioned."

Besides the tribe you want "High Contact Adults" (HCA pronounced Hayka). This would be coaches, youth pastors, instructors, etc. You also want to list Tribe Frequented Places (TFP pronounced Tifp). This would be the pizza joint, the gym, and the burger joint etc. Unfortunately most parking lots, back lots and dirt roads are unlisted.

Be creative with this. If you can't get this all filled out in one sitting then spread it out. If your teen tries to dodge you then put a consequence on it. Perhaps a simple statement like, "If this all isn't filled out by Friday I won't need these numbers because you wont be going out that weekend, I'll just have to call downstairs if I want you." Approach tribe member directly to get the information you have every right to ask for.

The simple act of asking for and getting this information is powerful. If you loose this sheet the day after it is completely filled out you have accomplished much. Think about it and it will make sense. Run off several copies befoe you start filling it out.

R.5

"Tribe Tracker"

Name_____

Home Phone _____

Mobile Phone _____

Car/Make/Model/License _____

Parents Name _____

Street Address _____

Name_____

Home Phone _____

Mobile Phone _____

Car/Make/Model/License _____

Parents Name _____

Street Address _____

Name_____

Home Phone _____

Mobile Phone _____

Car/Make/Model/License _____

Parents Name _____

Street Address _____

Name_____

Home Phone _____

Mobile Phone _____

Car/Make/Model/License _____

Parents Name _____

Street Address _____

Name_____

Home Phone _____

Mobile Phone _____

Car/Make/Model/License _____

Parents Name _____

Street Address _____

Name_____

Home Phone _____

Mobile Phone _____

Car/Make/Model/License _____

Parents Name _____

Street Address _____

Name_____

Home Phone _____

Mobile Phone _____

Car/Make/Model/License _____

Parents Name _____

Street Address _____

Name_____

Home Phone _____

Mobile Phone _____

Car/Make/Model/License _____

Parents Name _____

Street Address _____

Tribe Frequented Place _____

Phone _____

Address _____

Hours _____

Tribe Frequented Place _____

Phone _____

Address _____

Hours _____

High Contact Adults _____

Role_____ Number_____

High Contact Adults _____

Role_____ Number_____

Have a good time but, No swearing, No touching and No drugs

Curfew Contract Instructions

When setting curfew times make them concrete. Make sure that everyone understands how time can be gained or lost. Make sure that the contract emphasizes the child's behavior and how the **child** controls curfew time and freedom in general. Ensure the child that the more he meets expectations the less he will be monitored. Trust is earned. If you have already lost curfew credibility then set the base time one and one half ours before what curfew used to be. If the child does earn additional time then you must honor that. If you sign it then you must honor any positive initiatives on his part. The behaviors that are being used to earn or lose time must be measurable and definable. Unclear guideline - If Joey is disrespectful to his mother he will lose one hour off base time. What is "disrespectful?" It means different things to you and your child. Better guideline - If Joey shouts at his mother he will lose one hour off base time. Ok, this is better because we all know what a shout is so there can be no debate if he blows it. Best guideline example - If Joey shouts at and walks away from his mother while she is talking, then he will lose one hour off base time each time he does it. This is better because you moved from a vague description, "disrespectful," to actions that can be observed and noted. The same must be said for positive guidelines for granting additional time. Bad guideline - Joey will do better at school. Better - Joey will get a B average. Best - If Joey gets a B average on progress and report cards, then he will get an additional hour added to base time.

You get the idea. Make indicators for earning or losing time measurable or concrete. Do not feel that you must use this template or follow instructions exactly. Just do *something* to control the "window" of unsupervised time. Having too much freedom too soon is a common characteristic of children that are sexually active. Whatever you come up with, put it in writing. You'll sleep better.

Having too much freedom too soon is a common characteristic of children that are sexually active.

Curfew Contract For _____

(Teen's)_____ base time will be _____

on school nights and _____on non-school nights. Teen must be

able to give locations and numbers for each hour he is out past (base time) _____

If teen can give exact location, activity, and phone numbers for evening then he will get an

additional _____ after base time. However, contact information must be

exact for anytime allotted after base times. If group is co-ed than base time will be moved up

_____. Contact information will be held to a

higher standard whenever group is coed. (Teen)_____ will

lose _____ hour off base time for the following week whenever he _____

_____.

Teen can also lose _____ hour as a result of _____. Teen can

gain an additional _____hour(s) by _____.

Teen can also gain an additional _____hour(s) by _____.

All parties signed below agree to uphold the above contract. Any violation of contract will result
in decreased freedoms on the part of teen as well as _____hour(s) being taken off base time.

SIGNED

_____ Date _____

_____ Date _____

_____ Date _____

_____ Date _____

I use "If . . . Then" statements when dealing with my teen(s)

Purity Covenant

I hereby commit that I will not degrade myself and women by viewing pornography. I will not insult my future wife (or wife) by viewing images in comparison to her. I will be a man by controlling my eyes and therefore my desire. If I do fall into pornographic temptation I will confess it to my "band of brothers" and seek their encouragement and guidance.

Signature: _____ Date: _____

Witnesses: _____

_____

_____

_____

_____

There are three things which the superior man guards against. In youth - lust. When he is strong - quarrelsomeness. When he is old - covetousness.
– Confusious

Love looks not with the eyes, but with the mind.
– William Shakespeare

The Ten Computer Commandments

1 Thou shall not use the computer to view pornography.

2 Thou shall not use the computer to transmit or receive sexual imagery.

3 Thou shalt report any unasked for messages that contain sexual imagery to your parents. (It's not your fault if something nasty comes in while you're online if you didn't ask for it).

4 Thou shall not enter any unapproved chat rooms.

5 Thou shall not give out personal information (address, phone number, parents hours, etc.)

6 Thou shall not use a computer to bear false witness.

7 Thou shall not meet a computer contact face to face without a parent present.

8 Thou shall not use the computer to harm other people.

9 Thou shall not use computer resources without permission.

10 You shall use the computer in ways that show respect for yourself and honor your parents and your family.

The signers agreeth to followeth all commands or be eternally separated from computoreth.

_____ Date _____

_____ Date _____

_____ Date _____

_____ Date _____

Acknowledgement of Impact Contract

Girls who have a distant or no relationship with their father are two and one half times more likely to experience a teen pregnancy. Girls that do not feel loved or 'deemed worthy' by their fathers are two and one half times more likely to engage in risky sexual behavior.

initial

I have read and understand
the above concept _____

Above statement should be signed by biological father as well as stepfather, where applicable. Signed form should be stored in secure location in case risky sexual behavior does occur on the part of teen daughter and father complains about cost of counseling, termination of education, drug use and medical therapy associated with said behavior. Document should also be stored in the case teen conception does take place and father complains about cost associated with delivery, medications, and general support of daughter and baby. This additional budget expense may result in loss of bass boat or other toys.

Myth Bashing

To be completed by teen with guardian supervision. Read *Myth, Truth and Evidence* **statements and initial that you understand. Sign after reviewing completed document.**

Myth: STDs are rare at my school and within my tribe.

Truth: STDs are very common amongst *middle* and *high* school students in every community in America amongst *every* race and income group. Middle and high students are getting diseases even if they have not had sexual intercourse because many diseases can be spread through oral sex or genital contact. One out of four sexually active teenagers *have* a sexually transmitted disease. The majority of them don't know it because many of these diseases are asymptomatic (they have no symptoms). So, many middle and high school students are unaware that they are walking around with ticking time bombs inside them like chlamydia or herpes. They may be infected with herpes without having experienced their first outbreak. Many healthy teens can be infected for years without experiencing symptoms. ____ **Initial**

Evidence: One in ten teenage girls have chlamydia. (National Center for HIV, STD and TB Prevention, Centers for Disease Control, U.S. Department of Health and Human Services. "Tracking the Hidden Epidemics.") http:www.cdc.gov ___ **Initial**

Evidence: One in four sexually active teens has herpes, HPV or chlamydia. The majority are unaware of their condition. ("STDs in America: *How Many Cases and at What Cost?*" 1998, *Menlo Park, CA. Kaiser Family Foundation and American Social Health Association.*) ____ **Initial**

Evidence: Many people with chlamydia infections do not know they are infected. 85 percent of females and 40 percent of males who are infected have no symptoms. *Eng TR, Butler WT, eds. The Hidden Epidemic-Confronting Sexually Transmitted Disease. Institute of Medicine. Washington, DC: National Academy Press; 1997*___ **Initial**

Myth: Using condoms will eliminate the risk of getting a sexually transmitted disease.

Truth: Condoms have been shown to *reduce* the risk of pregnancy and diseases that must be transported in fluid (semen or vaginal secretion). However, condoms have been shown to be of little or no effect against diseases that can be contracted through skin to skin contact. This is because condoms cover only a small area of the surfaces that come into contact during oral, vaginal, or anal sex. ____ **Initial**

Evidence: Condoms *reduce* the transmission of HIV/ AIDs. There is *not* enough evidence to state that they are effective in reducing the risk of most other sexually transmitted diseases. *National Institute of Allergy and Infectious Diseases, National Institutes of Health, Department of Health and Human Services, Workshop Summary: Scientific Evidence On Condom Effectiveness for Sexually Transmitted Disease Prevention, July 20, 2001* ____ **Initial**

Evidence: Condoms have no impact on the risk of sexual transmission of human papilloma virus in women and there is no clear evidence that condoms reduce HPV transmission in men. *("Federal Panel on Condoms Offers Crucial Warnings to Sexually Active Americans, Says the Medical Institute for Sexual health" NIH Condom Reports, The Medical Institute for Sexual health, July 19, 2001.)* ____ **Initial**

Evidence: Current evidence does not show that Trichomonas vaginalis sexual transmission is reduced even with 100 percent condom use. *Ahmed S. Lutalo T. Wawer M, it al. HIV incidence and sexually transmitted disease prevalence associated with condom use: A population study in Rakai, Uganda:* ____ **Initial**

Myth: Oral sex is not sex and you cannot get a disease from oral sex.

Truth: Oral sex involves intimate physical contact and indeed *qualifies* as sex. Many diseases can be spread through penis to mouth or mouth to vaginal contact. Diseases like herpes and chlamydia can easily be transferred during oral sex even if a condom is being used. ____ **Initial**

Evidence: It is believed that oral sex was the transmission activity for 75% of new cases of herpes. The majority of young people that catch herpes catch it as a result of oral sex. *(Teens Say Oral Sex 'Doesn't Count' as more Engage. LifeDate, Spring 2001 issue. Internet on-line. www.lutheransforlife.org/lifedate 2001)* ____ **Initial**

Myth: Adopting an A.B.I. (Anything But Intercourse) approach will keep me safe from disease.

Truth: Avoiding intercourse does reduce your chance of getting a sexually transmitted disease. However, engaging in other sexual activities at the exclusion of intercourse still puts you at risk! Many diseases can be transferred through penis to mouth or mouth to vagina contact. Any contact with skin areas that are carrying diseases such as chlamydia, herpes, and HPV can result in contraction. ____ **Initial**

Evidence: HPV is spread through skin-to-skin contact and does not need vaginal/oral penetration or ejaculation to be transferred. *Division of STD Prevention. Prevention of genital HPV infection and squelae: Report of an external consultant's meeting. Department of Health and Human Services, Atlanta: Centers for Disease Control and Prevention (CDC), December 1999.*
____ **Initial**

Evidence: Herpes can be an oral as well as a genital infection. It can be spread by kissing and then spread to the genitals by oral sex. Herpes may infect hands, thighs, and abdomen. *Fleming DT, McQuillan GM, Johnson RE, et al. Herpes simplex virus type 2 in the United States, 1976 to 1994. N Engl J Med. 1997;337: 1105-1111* ____ **Initial**

Teen Signature_____ **Date** _____

Witness_____ **Date** _____

Waiting Until Marriage
Pledge Certificate

I make this commitment, before those that love me, that I will remain sexually abstinent from this day forward. That I will save myself for the one that cherishes me and pledges to spend his/her life with me. I will wait to experience the joys of sex until I'm in a committed, lifelong, marriage.

Signed: _____

Date: _____

Witness _____

Witness _____

The Heavy Hitters

There are currently 45 sexually transmitted diseases making the rounds in the Untied states. HPV, Chlamydia, and herpes are the ones that your teen is most at risk of contracting. Aids is included in the list because, though your teen is less likely to be exposed to it, it is still the most deadly.

Human Papilloma Virus (HPV)

HPV is a virus that infects skin and mucous membranes ((tissues that line the mouth, cervix, vagina, urethra and anus) of humans. Transmission occurs through sexual intercourse, oral sex, and genital touching. Most people have no symptoms. Most females discover they have HPV when a Pap smear reveals abnormalities. HPV is not curable. The long-term effects of HPV in woman can be disastrous. HPV is the primary cause of over 99 percent of cervical cancers. Because HPV is spread by skin-to-skin contact condoms are ineffective due to the fact that they do not cover the whole genital area. Abstinence is the best protection from HPV.

Chlamydia

Chlamydia is the most common bacterial sexually transmitted Disease in America. It is transmitted through sexual activity. Currently 10 percent of teen girls are infected with Chlamydia. The vast majorities do not know they are infected. If there are symptoms they are typically vaginal or urethral discharge, burning with urination, pelvic pain in women, and swelling and tenderness of the scrotum in men. If a chlamydia infection remains undetected long enough, it may lead to a potentially fatal disease called pelvic inflammatory disease (PID). Chlamydia is usually diagnosed when symptoms prompt the infected person to get examined. If the clinician checks genital fluids or urine for it, it can be easily detected. Chlamydia infections in both men and women are typically treated with oral antibiotics. The long-term effects are PID and infertility as well as tubul scarring and increased risks for subsequent entopic (tubal) pregnancy. Long-term Chlamydia infections have been linked to infertility.

Genital Herpes

Genital Herpes is a virus that infects the skin and mucous membranes of the mouth, and genital areas. It is the most common sexually transmitted virus in the United States. The symptoms can be lessoned with medication. However, it cannot be cured. Herpes can be spread through sexual intercourse, oral sex, and mutual masturbation and kissing. In addition to herpes infection in the genital and oral areas, it may also occur on the thighs, hands, and abdomen. Initial symptoms include fever, headache and muscle ache that usually occur six to ten days after exposure. Onset may initially be lesions. However, these lesions usually progress to painful ulcers that itch and burn.

HIV and AIDS

HIV can only be transferred through contact with infected blood, semen, vaginal secretions or breast milk. The virus enters through the anus and vagina, breast milk, pregnancy or delivery and a break or sore in the skin. One of the greatest problems in combating this disease is the fact that you can be infected and still have a negative blood test. In other words, a teen can become infected at fifteen, test negative until 25, and infect many of his/her partners before detection. Aids is still deadly. It will still kill. The new medications out have delayed death from aids, not prevented it. Because this disease must have an exchange of body fluid to be contracted, condoms do marginally reduce (but not eliminate) the risk of exposure.

APPENDIX C

Toolbox

Note: I am recommending these tools based on my experiences with them, impact on topic, and usability. If you find a service or product you feel would be useful that is not on this list, by all means buy it. I provide this list at the risk of leaving some great tools out of the toolbox. I decided to provide it anyway. I know that as a parent you struggle with time and I felt you would be more likely to use additional materials if I did some of the searching for you. If cost is a challenge please see "Group buying" section in Study Question Chapter. I have no financial relationship with any of the people, organizations, or resources listed below except for my own products and services.

ORGANIZATIONS AND WEB SITES THAT CAN HELP

National Abstinence Clearing House
801 E. 41st Street, Sioux Falls, SD 57105
Ph: 605-335-3643 Fax: 605-335-0629
Email: info@abstinence.net Web site www.abstinence.net
The definitive resource encompassing articles, speakers, events and resource directory

Keith's Notes - They are just what their blurb says. They are an international clearing house for abstinence everything. Not only that but they are great people!
Keith's Gotta Have - The "Faces of Abstinence Calendar" You must get this for your teen's room. It is a cool, in, hip, bad, and vibrant calendar that features pictures of attractive young people and their testimonies on why they have chosen to remain abstinent until marriage. Some of former features were Miss America and Miss Black America winners as well as high school and college young men and women. If these kids can put their first and last names and big glossy picture on a calendar they know is going to be distributed nationally then your kid will feel encouraged to make his/her own stand. Call 1.888.57SAYNO (7-2966)
Keith's Also Gotta Have - If your child has been sexually active, then while you are on the phone order the brochure, "Secondary Virginity" for thirty cents. It's to the point and encouraging at the same time.

WWW.moviemom.com
http://movies.yahoo.com/moviemom

This web site is written specifically for parent to research current, upcoming, and past movies. The ratings system is not specific enough. This site provides detailed information on sexual content, language, and violence as well as overall theme. DVD releases are also covered. Moviemom also allows browsers to search its database for age appropriate movies.

FamilyCow.com
www.familycow.com

Practical tools to help protect your family against TV obscenity and Internet pornography. Great site. **Has additional tools for TV control not mentioned in body of my book.** They feature sharp products like the weemote; a TV remote control for kids that let them see only the channels their parents choose. They offer TVAllowance. That's right. This device lets you allot each child a number of hours and when they use them up...Mr. TV will not come on for them. Much more. These items are not exclusive to this site. What this site does is put them all together for you and explain them in a manner a technophobe would understand.

Filter Review
www.internetfilterreview.com

This site provides overview and explanation of nit filter option. It ranks filters by various functions and saves parents the time it would take to investigate individual filter sites. The user will be walked through a step-by-step process of researching, deciding, and buying an Internet filter that is a good fit for their family.

ABC's of the Birds and Bees for Parents of Toddlers to Teens
Aim for Success, Inc.
www.aimforsuccess.org

Marilyn Morris, President of Aim for Success, Inc., provides answers to the 50 most frequently asked questions parents want to know regarding their children and sex.

How At Risk Are You
Why Know Abstinence Education, Inc.
www.whyknow.org

This inexpensive and popular pamphlet is a great teaching tool. The sexual exposure chart graphically reveals a sexually active teen's true vulnerability to sexually transmitted disease. Your teen doesnít have to read a word. All he has to do is look at the chart to understand the risks he may be taking.

Sexual Exposure Chart
Why know Abstinence Education, Inc.
www.whyknow.org

This inexpensive 16" by 20" poster will get your teen's (and their tribe's) attention. Once starting sexual activity, research shows that teens are likely to have more than one partner. There is a scientific concept that is easily expressed to teens with this sentence, "When you have sex with someone, you are exposed to every person your partner has had sex with." The short version is, "When you have sex you are having sex with every person that person has had sex with." From a medical standpoint, we know that STDs can remain undetected or asymptomatic for long periods. In other words the disease from previous partners can live in one person. That one person can then pass on multiple diseases from multiple previous partners, to their current partner. This is a great tool for parents of those on the brink of sexual activity or those teens that respond to the abstinence message with, "I'm not sleeping around, I'm just with 'Billy.'" (I call this the "one partner" defense). This poster shows that you are exposed to all the partners that your partner has been exposed to. As I mentioned in the body of my book (Myth Bashing or Dog Poop Proposal), explaining is not as powerful as showing. This poster is powerful.

What They Never Told You
Abstinence Education Council
www.savesex.net

Another great inexpensive ($.45) poster that artistically lists the consequences of premarital sex and the advantages of abstinence.

Abstinence Survival Kit
Abstinence Clearing House
www.abstinence.net

This is a resource for those of you that want to take this message to the community. This manual teaches you how to understand the philosophy of abstinence education verses that of comprehensive (condoms are the answer) sexed. This book gives practical advice on how to work with school boards and area policy makers to in order to get an abstinence-until-marriage program in your school system.

Note - Though several of the books listed may appear to contradict in approach they all promote sexual abstinence until marriage and a fulfilling sex life afterward.

What a Difference a Daddy Makes
The Indelible Imprint a Dad Leaves on His Daughter's Life
Dr. Kevin Leman
Thomas Nelson Publishers

Wow, a book that focuses exclusively on the relationship between fathers and daughters. Though there are many books on fathering, there are precious few that focus on the critical father daughter relationship. This book does a great job. As I mentioned in my book, each chapter or issue that we took on in of itself deserves a whole book. If you want to explore the father daughter relationship more closely, this would be the book. Most importantly, Leman looks at the outcomes that DADD; (Daddy Attention Deficit Disorder) will bring about. A wake up call for any father who doesn't understand how important he is to his little girl. If Dad just reads the first three chapters and falls back under the trance of ESPN, it will still do your daughter some good.

Protecting The Gift
KEEPING CHILDREN AND TEENAGERS SAFE (AND PARENTS SANE)
Gavin De Becker
The Dial Press

This book will save lives. It's that simple. This book does not deal with promoting abstinence. Why include it? Because it promotes protecting children. De Becker provides practical solutions for keeping children safe in a violence prone America. You will learn how to protect your child from baby sitters and nannies, being away from home, sexual predators, school situations, guns and other family members. Yes, you worry about pedophiles and perhaps even some of the adult members of your extended family. Now you can do something besides worry. The book is chilling but at the same time empowering. You have the tools and the instincts you need to protect your children. The book is riveting. In my work with families I have often implored parents to "go with their gut instinct" when considering visitation rights, boyfriends, or suspicious behavior. Now I will give them this book. I will leave you with a quote from de Becker from the inside cover, "I commit that by the end of this book, you'll know more and be uncertain less; see more and deny less, accept more and hesitate less; act more and worry less." Get the book.

Life and Death on the Internet
How to Protect Your Family on the World Wide Web
Keith A. Schroeder

Most in depth (in my opinion) book on Internet safety. It may be too in-depth for some readers. Solutions are given in a step by step manner. This book provides filtering information that is found in many other net safety books. Additionally Schroeder includes directions to find hidden files and to purge unwanted files. You will also learn how to detect what your child has been "doing" and where he has "gone" on the internet. Schroeder not only shows you how to protect your children but also how to make sure all your personal and private information stays confidential. Parents should be aware that this is not a book that should be left lying around the home. The author provides an appendix that lists all the free and anonymous pornographic newsgroups. He does this so you can better "fight back". However, these are not addresses that should be in the hands of children or adults that struggle with pornography. If you have a technological savvy teen that knows more about the Internet than any of your friends that work with computers, then, this is the "Internet book" you need to buy. Perhaps I can give you a better indicator if this should be your Internet Safety book. If you have a child that can create his own web page or play real time role playing games then you need this book.

THE PLEDGE EVENT

Can an event be a tool? Of course. A tool is defined as something that helps you do work. Pledge events have been shown to have a tremendous impact on the pledgers sexual behavior. I have taken part in hundreds of these since 1993. It is still incredibly exciting to see hundreds of kids crammed into a coliseum or gym committing to abstinence until marriage. A pledge event is simply a time where teens come together and make a public commitment to sexual abstinence. There is a multitude of ways to do this but at the core must be gathering as large a group as possible, and making a public commitment. I strongly recommend using pledge cards. A goal or pledge is much more powerful when written down. The cards can then be posted in a public place.

As stated earlier, there are organizations that can also provide pledge cards and promo material. You don't have to use any organization if you don't want to. Just remember an abstinence rally without a call for a public commitment to abstinence is not powerful. It will just be one more "Youth Event." The youth must stand up and be counted. They should fill out pledge cards or go through some outward sign that they are making a commitment to abstinence. You may choose to fill out the pledge certificate (R.15) after the pledge event.

How wonderful it is that nobody need wait a single moment before starting to improve the world.
—Anne Frank

APPENDIX D

Group Study Questions

To best use the power of "group" study and implement at the same time.

Group Instructions

These questions are formatted so that you should be able to (at the next meeting) read and answer one chapter per week. As a group you may decide to go faster or slower. Besides acting as a study group the group may also act as a support system. The ideal situation would be for a group of parents to study and implement each chapter at the same time. Then the members would be able to encourage advise and share information on each of the strategies in the book. For example, if the entire study group did "the talk" together (chapter eleven) over the same week they would be able to compare notes at the next meeting. A parent team may have had great success with "the talk" while another may have crashed and burned. The "successful team" can then encourage and share the approach they used. Likewise group members can share "discoveries". If the whole group is dealing with the Internet at the same time (chapter eight) then perhaps a group member that is computer savvy can help and encourage the group. Or a group member may share the address of a filterware program that worked well for them.

From Chapter 4 to Chapter 14, each group session should contain two components: discussion of the implementation of the previous week's lesson and discussion of the next week's assignment. "How did it go?" and then "what do we do next?"

The last questions for Chapters 4 through 14 are, "What is on your "Action Plan?" And "Why?" If you share with a group what you have decided to do you are more likely to do it. You are also going to get additional ideas and encouragement. Fill in your action plans and share. This book is only worth the time and money you spent on it if some type of change takes place as a result of reading it. You are more likely to make changes if you write down the actions that will be required to create change (action plan). And you are even more likely to carry out those actions if you share what you wrote with a group of people (study group sessions).

Chapter 1

1. Why is Denial so tempting?_____

2. Is Denial deadly, why or why not? _____

3. Give an example of a cultural icon, politician or sports figure that fell under the seduction of denial. What was the result?_____

4. Can we be seduced into a state of denial? If so, what forces seduce us into denial?

   _____

5. Keith believes that this denial of sexual risk in our home is coupled with an abdication of responsibility. What is the responsibility he is talking about? _____

   _____

6. Do you believe that it is a parent's responsibility to form their child's worldview? Is this something that is best left to the child to figure out?_____

   _____

7. Is their even a "right and wrong" to sex? Do you feel the idea of promoting Virginity is not workable? Why or why not? _____

   _____

8. Are you in denial?_____

Chapter 2

1. In your own words, what is Parental Learned Helplessness? _____

   _____

2. Why is it important that we feel confident when dealing with our child's sexual behavior?

   _____

3. Give an example of how you may have been "shocked." What forces or events have given you a feeling of being temporarily or permanently overwhelmed? _____

   _____

4. What would be some probable outcomes for his people if Winston Churchill had not overcome his case of Learned Helplessness? _____

5. Do you feel overwhelmed by our sex-saturated culture? Can you give a specific example of sex-saturation in our culture that you find particularly bothersome? _____

6. Have you ever gone with the flow in regards to accepting pornography or sex saturation in your environment? _____

Chapter 3

1. In your own words, what is this chapter about and how does it relate to protecting your child's sexual purity. _____

2. Is there precedent for, "doing the right thing" despite potential conflict? _____
_____

3. The first three chapters of this book focus on your thought process regarding your roll in guiding your child's sexual worldview. Do you feel that these three chapters are overstated? Does Keith exaggerate the importance of recognizing the threat, recognizing that you can influence sexual behavior and being willing to deal with conflict? Do you feel it is appropriate to start a book on teen abstinence with these topics? Have you had to address the way you think about these three issues? _____
_____

4. Do you believe that disciplining is showing love towards a child? Why or why not?_____
_____

5. Will viewing discipline as an expression of love raise your confidence to discipline?_____
_____

6. Keith believes that sliding or giving in on the small stuff will lead to sliding on the big stuff. Do you agree?_____

7. Keith makes a connection between whether a child is in a permissive or disciplined home and their risk for teen sex. Do you agree that the connection is there or is this a stretch?
_____

8. Name a public figure that started off small in their lack of discipline and moved on to larger transgressions. See if you can isolate each step of the decline. _____
_____

9. Do you remember the "Pay me now or pay me later" oil filter commercials? Can you make a connection between those commercials and the relationship between discipline and sexual behavior.? _____
_____

Chapter 4

1. Do you agree that keeping your finger on the pulse of your teen's social life has a dramatic effect on their sexual risk level? _____

2. Keith is asking for a high level of monitoring. Will this be a challenge? What are some ways that a husband and wife could divide the workload that is required to stay on top of your

teen's social life? _____

3. How can divorced parents work together to implement the strategies outlined in Chapter 4.

   _____

4. Keith believes that you are communicating on many different levels when putting your child and the tribe through the wringer. Is this correct? What kinds of things may your teen be hearing? _____

5. What does Keith mean when he states, "the tribe has a collective conscience?"

   _____

6. At what point in American history did many American parents start believing that by closely monitoring their childís social life they were being "intrusive?"_____

   _____

7. Keith believes that sometimes parents decision-making processes are influenced by something he calls "dual income guilt." Do you believe there is such a thing? If so, do you believe that it can have a powerful influence on parentsí actions? _____

   _____

8. Many sexual encounters occur on weekdays after school before parents get home. What are some creative ways an individual family or community can make these few but dangerous hours safer? _____

9. What have you heard about in your teen's life that you did not respond adequately to?

   _____

10. As a class set up a hypothetical child in a hypothetical family. Make up a history for that child. Then describe a series of stages or events that would eventually lead to sexual intercourse. What were the warning signs? What did the early stages for your hypothetical child look like?

    _____

11. What is on your action plan? Why? _____

Chapter 5

1. These first two strategies are simple. Are they too simple? Do you believe that opening your house to the tribe will decrease the risk of sexual activity for your teen?_____

2. When you were a teen, where did you hang out, what did you do on a Friday night when you weren't at home, at the movies, or at a restaurant? How have the risks of "hanging out" changed?_____

3. In your own words what does the statement, "Their desire to socialize in groups may drive them to a location where sex is possible" mean?_____

4. By setting aside a room in the house and inviting the tribe in, what type of statement are you making besides the obvious?_____

5. What are some other ways besides those mentioned in the chapter to lure or entice the tribe into your house?_____

6. Would you feel comfortable if your gathering begins to grow into a youth outreach? Why or why not?_____

7. What do you think Keith meant by a "no sexual pressure zone." Do you believe that kids may actually feel unpressured hanging out at your house?_____

8. Studies show that many sexual encounters occur in the teen's home when parents are not present. Is inviting coed groups of teens into your house sending the wrong message? Or, by your being there, are you sending the right message? How can you let teens know that they are not welcome when you are not home?_____

9. How do you feel about what Keith calls "the newest stupid parent trick," the coed sleep over? This is the newest trend amongst "cool and hip" parents. What message do you feel young people are getting if they are allowed to sleep over in coed groups, even it they are closely monitored?_____

10. If you have started working on this strategy or constructing your room share your ideas and experiences with the class. _____

11. What is on your action plan? Why?_____

Chapter 6

1. In you own words list the five benefits of setting a curfew. How do these relate to lowering the risk of teen sex?_____

2. In your own words define, "window of exposure." _____

3. Why is it better to have teens "earn" curfews than to set them according to age or grade level?_____

4. Why do Bob and Beth present the curfew plan together? What is the "fundamental shift in power" that Bucky observes?_____

5. Why is it important to "write it down?" _____

6. Can the "if/then" approach be used on all the other strategies in this book?_____

7. The if/then approach is all about consequences. Do you believe, as Keith does, that there is an alarming trend occurring within American parenting to "rescue" teens from experiencing

the negative consequences brought about by their poor decisions? Keith believes that making teens "pay the consequences" for their own bad decisions will better equip them to handle the decision to become sexually active or not. Do you agree with this? Why or why not?

_____

8. What is on your action plan? Why?_____

Chapter 7

1. What exactly, does the "Hickory Dickory Dock" exercise prove? _____

2. Do you believe what teen's see and hear can affect their sexual behavior? Why or Why not?

_____

3. Keith believes that this will be one of the strategies that parents will be the most reluctant to implement. Do you agree with him? Why or why not? _____

4. The average teen watches 23 hours of TV per week. Does this surprise you? How many hours do you think your teen watches? Do you feel you may be under estimating?

_____

5. Using the statistics given, find out how much TV the average 2 - 11 year old and the average teen watch in a year. Convert the hours to days. Express the final answer for both in days.

_____

6. Keith believes that the industries involved with media are suppressing the studies that connect viewing to negative behaviors. Do you agree with him? Why or why not. _____

_____

7. Before reading this book, did you believe that marriage is under assault? Do you believe it now or to you think Keith is using reactionary or inflammatory language?

_____

8. Were you aware that popular mainstream music contains lyrics like, "I got changed and I'm sitting on the side of Satan" or "I just took some ecstasy- all these fine bitches mean sex to me, plus I got this bad bitch layin next to me - sit back on the couch, pants down, rubber on, set to turn that ass out, laid the bitch out, then I put it in her mouth?"_____

9. Keith focuses the later part of this chapter on males. Do you think this focus is warranted? Why or why not?_____

10. What is on your action plan? Why? _____

_____

Chapter 8

1. Describe the approach of "divide and conquer" that is referred to throughout chapters seven, eight and nine. In your own words what does Keith mean by "device" and what does he mean by "content?" _____

2. Do you believe that simply moving the computer to a more public place can have the positive impact that Keith describes? _____

3. How can teens be exposed to sexually explicit materials without looking for them?

   _____

4. During the early teen years young boys are forming their ideas about their gender and the role sex plays in relationships. How would the repetitive viewing of hardcore online pornography affect a young boy's perception of women and sex? _____

5. Will you actually do the "Dog Poop Proposal?" Why or why not? If you will not do it can you join with another family in your group that will? Perhaps two families can get together and have a cookout. _____

   _____

6. Dealing with the Internet and making sure you are protected can be very frustrating. Pool your resources. If there is a member of the group that is "good at computer stuff" then perhaps you can have them over for dinner or work out a "barter." Poll the group. Is there anybody who is comfortable with the Internet and filterware. Has this book brought about conflict and fatigue? Are the strategies Keith is asking you to implement robbing you of time and health? Is this all worth it? _____

   _____

7. By this time, you must be realizing that battling sex saturated teen media is going to be a difficult and extracted struggle. Can you think of a parent in your community or personal experience that struggled long and hard on a different front for their child? Perhaps you can recall a parent that had to deal with health, marital, or financial difficulties. What do you think kept this parent "going to bat" for their child? Do you have some of those same qualities? _____

   _____

8. What is on your action plan? Why? _____

   _____

Chapter 9

1. Certain parenting groups came out against Elvis and the Beatles. Have we simply turned into our parents? Have you ever heard or read statements like, "They said our music was bad and we came out 'ok'. Why should we bother them about their music." Or, "Our parents said the

same thing about the Stones. It's just the some stuff we used to listen to, but it sounds different." Are these statements accurate? Is some of the teen music Keith mentions as damaging as he says it is? _____

2. Are you just stepping into the role of, "Restrictive, Ignorant, Controlling Parent" (RICP) pronounced Ricp) when you seek input on music choices? _____

3. What aspects of Keith's strategy can help you from being painted into an anti art corner? What things does Keith ask you to do in order to keep yourself from being labeled a Restrictive, Ignorant, and Controlling Parent? _____

4. Keith believes that when you eliminate a negative habit you must replace it with a positive habit. Do you agree? Or is it possible to take the most damaging music without plugging in positive music? Can you eliminate "death rock" without putting in "life rock?"_____

_____

5. Why is it more important to attack the negative lyrics rather than the sound of the music?

_____

6. The band, Slipknot, throw their own feces at each other and drink their own urine while onstage. One of their songs includes the lyrics: "Insane, am I the only motherfucker with a brain? I'm hearing voices but all they do is complain, how many times have you wanted to kill, everything and everyone, say you'll do it but never will." Can you think of a band or lyrics from the 70s or 80s that had similar lyrics and stage behavior? _____

7. The popular band, Insane clown Posse, sing: "I feel I'd rather kill you, cuz I got you in my car, you ain't goin' nowhere bitch, you're dead, I'd rather cut that neck in half, I'd rather choke out that bitch ass I would rather bang your head on the wall until you fall into a coma." Do you feel that this type of song could have a negative effect on the nationsí teens or have we just turned into our parents complaining about the Rolling Stones?_____

8. As a class, role-play the call Keith encourages you to make. Call the parents of another household and inform them of your media guidelines. Role play several times until you find the words that work best for you. Do this until you feel comfortable making "the call" Make the real call over the week and report the results. If the opportunity does not present itself then report the result when the opportunity does. _____

9. What is on your action plan? Why?_____

Group Ordering . . . As a class turn to the TOOLBOX section. Go through and discuss. Pick different tools that appeal to you. If you order these tools they will arrive by the time you complete this study guide. You will save time and money by group ordering. Each person in the class order or buy (several of the books are available at brick and mortar stores at this time) a tool. Make sure nobody orders the same tool. At your last session you are going to have an "abstinence fair". You are going to do an adult version of show and tell. Each member will bring in a "tool" and share it with the class. Isn't this exciting? Then the members of the class will find out if a tool is right for them without purchasing the tool. You may then trade back and forth. Obviously, you are not going to trade calendars or posters back and forth. But you get the idea. If you see something you like, order it. You may also want to order catalogues from each different organization listed in the TOOLBOX.

Want greater impact? Present a Community-wide Abstinence Fair.

Cover several folding tables with attractive material and display to the whole community. Make it simple for people to order what is on display. The effort you put into this could change lives dramatically.

Schedule your class-wide abstinence fair for the session after you finish the questions for chapter fourteen. Schedule your community-wide fair for whenever you can get it through committee or neighborhood association.

Chapter 10

1. In your own words, what is chapter ten about and how is it related to your teen's sexual behavior? Can you express this relationship in one sentence? _____

2. What is the fear that some parents have? Have you ever felt this fear? _____

3. Why is it important that we address this fear?_____

4. Studies show that parents today spend 40% less time with their children than the generation before them. Do you feel this is relevant to the increase in teen sexual activity? _____

5. Do you feel that feeling guilty about the lack of time spent with teens can lead to permissive parenting? Can permissive parenting lead to early sexual activity in teens?_____

6. Do you ever feel guilty about the amount of time you spend with your children? Do you acknowledge this guilt in your upper mind or is it "down there somewhere"? Do you think guilt about time decisions could be affecting your parenting style without you even being aware of it? Why or why not?_____

7. In our society, time has become the ultimate prestige symbol. Americans are the people who came up with the slogan; "time is money". Do you agree that time is treasure? Is it possible to be greedy with time? After all, time is not a thing, is it?_____

8. What is on your action plan? Why?_____

Note: Do not have the talk outlined in chapter eleven until completing the role playing session.

Chapter 11

1. Have you had "the talk" prior to reading this book? If so, how did it go?_____

2. Why does "the talk" have to have more to it than, "Don't have sex, you could get a disease or get (somebody) pregnant?"_____

3. Has it occurred to you to have the talk, but you put it off? Why?_____

4. Keith quotes research that the talk actually makes a difference when coupled with ongoing dialogue. Do you believe this? What qualifies as ongoing dialogue?_____

5. Break up into groups of three and role-play. Have "two parents" and one "child." Go through the outline in Chapter 11. Have the child use different responses and different attitudes. Try to get the child to talk. Rotate so everyone gets to be parent or child.

6. Why is it important that this not become an anti-sex talk?_____

7. What are some things you can do to make sure it does not become an anti-sex talk?_____

_____

8. Besides prompts that Keith suggests in the chapter, what are some other ways to bring up sex in everyday living. Are there other ways besides the ones mentioned to reintroduce the topic after you have had the talk?_____

9. What is on your action plan? Why?_____

Chapter 12

1. Do you agree that aggressively educating your child about the true risks of STDs can have an affect on his sexual behavior?_____

2. Keith discussed the "four myths" in detail. In the following exercise your must come up with a one sentence response to each of the four myths. Your sentence should be a summary of your argument against the four myths and in support of the truth.

   "Oral sex is not sex." _____

   "Condoms will protect me." _____

   "Diseases are rare at my school." _____

   "Practicing A.B.I (Anything But Intercourse) will keep me safe." _____

3. How can you relate the "cause and effect" theme in chapter 6 to this chapter?

_____

4. Break into groups and try the responses to the four myths on one another. Try to graphically and logically counter the myths using information you have learned. Remember, if you don't feel uncomfortable, you are not using descriptive enough language.

5. . Share what is in your action plan? Why? _____

Chapter 13

1. Keith stated that prevention strategies in the book would progress from easy to tough. What is tough about this chapter? What is awkward about it? _____

2. The father daughter dynamic and its relationship to teen pregnancy is one of the most well-documented aspects of early female sexual behavior. Yet it is seldom addressed. Why is that?

_____

3. In your own words, how does a father influence a teen girls perspective of boys and men?

_____

4. In your own words, how does a distant or nonexistent relationship with father increase the likelihood of early sexual activity? _____

5. Why can a father who is not paying any attention to his daughter be more damaging than if the girl had no father present at all? _____

6. How can you get a distant dad to spend time with his daughter? _____

7. If there is no dad, and there will be no dad, what is the good news in this chapter for single moms? _____

8. Do you feel the role of "father" is respected in America? Why or Why not? _____

_____

9. Men are praised for being strong, handsome, athletic, good businessmen and artistic as well as many other attributes. Within public discourse, how often do you hear the comment, "He's a good father?"

10. What is on your action plan? Why? _____

_____

Chapter 14

1. Keith makes the statement; "If your teen is exposed to an unstable marriage then it invalidates everything you have to say about sex and love." Do you agree with this statement? Why or why not? _____

2. Keith believes that something called "home environment" can affect teen sexual behavior. Do you agree? Why or why not. _____

3. What is "home environment"? Do you have a healthy one? _____

4. In your own words, describe the relationship between your marriage and your teen's perception of sex and the role of sex within life? _____

5. Are you modeling something worth waiting for? _____

6. What are the three things you can start doing to present a better marital front to your teen?

   _____

7. In light of the importance of the health or your marriage and the influence that it has on your teen's sexual behavior, besides the three fixes Keith mentions what are some additional emergency fixes you can put in? _____

8. How often does your family eat together? In this survey eating together means everybody in the family sits down at a table together. _____

9. What radical step could be taken in order to increase eating together as a family? This may include such radical strategies as Dad preparing the meal or the teens preparing the meal.

   _____

Comedic Shows available from Keith Deltano

The Redneck Was Right

The Redneck Was Right is a hilarious and entertaining true story. Keith will take you on his journey through the U.S. Army Airborne School where he judged a fellow soldier with a background very different from his own. By showing how wrong his initial judgement was and how a wonderful friendship was eventually formed, Keith challenges the youth and adults in the audience to seriously contemplate how they look at one another. This show is about acceptance, the danger of cliques, and making new friends by reaching out. Keith shows how foolish it is to judge one another by outward appearance, speech, or economic status.

Abstinence is Cool

Abstinence is Cool is a show recommended for sixth through twelfth grade students. Keith will take this topic head on with humor, energy and facts. He will actually equip young people with things to say and do to help them handle the pressures of their peers and today's society. Abstinence is Cool will force the youth to confront the harsh risks of premarital sexual activity and promote abstinence until marriage and monogamy afterwards. In conjunction with the show, Keith can also conduct a workshop for parents called, Keeping Your Kid a Virgin 101. Great for pledge event.

Drugs Are Stupid

Keith uses his trademark high-energy approach to illustrate just how stupid drug use is. He takes on it all, from cigarettes to meth. Keith will "arrest" and "cuff" a drug user as well as "pull over" a drunk driver. Keith uses his knowledge of teen culture and language to get through to them that paying money for something that destroys them is just plain stupid.

I'm Dreaming Of A Stress Free Christmas

I*'m Dreaming of a Stress Free Christmas* is an eye opening show. Keith takes on the commercialization of Christmas: the marketing, the promotions, the malls, the parking, the decorations, and gifts we feel we must have and buy. The mandatory parties, hectic schedules, once a year cooking, strained family relations, and awkward gift situations all fall under his comic wit. He will also share ideas that can be used to reclaim Christmas for family and friends.

Discernment... Do I Really Need That?

Discernment . . . Do I Really Need That? challenges the audience to take a close look at what is really important in life and what is not. Keith takes a humorous look at dept, decision-making, priorities, and over scheduling. Great for adult only audiences or as part of financial and marriage seminars.

Whatever Happened to Marriage?

A humorous look into today's marriages and insights to make them better.

Don't Be Stupid

A unique approach to show teens the dangers of drug and alcohol abuse.

Custom for You

Keith will prepare a show specifically for your organization (time allowing)

To bring Keith in for performances contact Nashville Speakers Bureau at www.nashspeakers.com or call 1-866-333-8663 OR 1-615-236-1072

Notes . . .